Thinking with Kierkegaard and Wittgenstein

Thinking with Kierkegaard and Wittgenstein

The Philosophical Theology of Paul L. Holmer

Richard Griffith Rollefson

Foreword by
David J. Gouwens

☙PICKWICK *Publications* · Eugene, Oregon

THINKING WITH KIERKEGAARD AND WITTGENSTEIN
The Philosophical Theology of Paul L. Holmer

Pickwick Publications
An Imprint of Wipf and Stock Publishers
199 W. 8th Ave., Suite 3
Eugene, OR 97401

www.wipfandstock.com

ISBN 13: 978-1-4982-5674-2

Cataloguing-in-Publication Data

Rollefson, Richard Griffith.

Thinking with Kierkegaard and Wittgenstein : the philosophical theology of Paul L. Holmer / Richard Rollefson ; foreword by David J. Gouwens

xiv + 152 p. ; 23 cm. —Includes bibliographical references.

ISBN 13: 978-1-4982-5674-2

1. Holmer, Paul L. 2. Kierkegaard, Søren, 1813–1855. 3. Kierkegaard, Søren, 1813–1855—Religion. 4. Wittgenstein, Ludwig, 1889–1951. 5. Religion—Philosophy. I. Gouwens, David Jay. II. Title.

BJ1012 .R65 2014

Manufactured in the U.S.A.

Dedicated to
"That definite individual"
Paul L. Holmer

Contents

Foreword

Throughout his career at the University of Minnesota and Yale Divinity School, Paul L. Holmer was known as a master teacher, famed at Yale for his courses in philosophical theology, including "Readings in Kierkegaard," "Wittgenstein and Meaning," "Vices and Virtues," and "Emotions, Passions, and Feelings." In those courses, Holmer challenged his students to join him in the hard work of exploring philosophical and theological concepts such as language, meaning, understanding, knowledge, faith, certainty, ethics, belief, theology, and God. At the same time, Holmer challenged his students to consider carefully the deep interweaving of concepts and personal capacities, how our thinking must attend, as Richard Rollefson well puts it, to "the workings of ordinary language within the workings of a human life," "touching on the most fundamental and enduring issues of human life." Through his teaching as well as his writings, Holmer influenced several generations of philosophers, theologians, and ministers.

Despite his influence, Holmer's thought is not as well-known as it deserves. We can therefore be grateful to Richard Rollefson for providing us this first full-length book on Holmer's thought. Rollefson surveys a wide range of Holmer's books and essays, and the reader will find thoughtful orientation to some of Holmer's main publications, including *The Grammar of Faith*, *C.S. Lewis: The Shape of His Faith and Thought*, and *Making Christian Sense*. Further, Rollefson traces carefully the development of Holmer's thought, from his early engagement with Søren Kierkegaard under David F. Swenson's tutelage at the University of Minnesota, to Holmer's later assimilation of Ludwig Wittgenstein. But equally important, as Rollefson shows, Holmer uses these two figures to construct his own distinctive critical, non-foundational philosophical theology focusing on the logic of ethical and religious belief. In Holmer's understanding, philosophy and theology are best practiced not in developing large-scale metaphysical theories, or second-order typologies of schools of thought, but in investigating how our language finds its home within the complex of non-linguistic uses and practices that shape our lives. "Understanding" ethics and religious belief, in particular, requires patiently exploring the intersection of concept and capacity that forms the web of human life.

From his thorough familiarity with Holmer's writings, Rollefson also helps prevent some common misreadings of Holmer. Because of Holmer's stringent critiques, he has sometimes been labeled a "Wittgensteinian fideist," or "relativist," or a "positivist" rejecting all ontology and metaphysics. But Rollefson shows well how misleading are such characterizations of Holmer's thought, and how subtle and nuanced are Holmer's reflections on these matters.

Because of Holmer's concern for the intersection of language and life, concept and capacity, a central passion of Holmer's thought, Rollefson rightly claims, is the "morphology of the self." At stake for Holmer, he continues, were again not only the grammar of our language but the grammar of our lives. In his teaching and writing both, Holmer always conveys a bracing intellectual rigor with moral and religious earnestness.

That concern for the "morphology of the self," the "grammar" of our lives, combined with such religious earnestness, has sometimes been attributed to Holmer's Lutheran pietist background, but Rollefson shows how for Holmer that morphology is anything but anti-intellectualistic or a thoughtless advocacy of a "primacy of experience over reflection." As a thinker Holmer never rejected the importance of thought; he always saw Christian faith linked with Christian teaching and theology. But he did argue for an appreciation of how careful theological reflection is, at its best, rooted in ethical, religious, and Christian passion, in what Holmer called, echoing Kierkegaard, "a living synthesis of will, thought, and pathos, all three." Rollefson rightly emphasizes this deeply synthetic feature of Holmer's thought, which in turn displays Holmer as a profoundly humanist Christian thinker.

Holmer was always suspicious of attempts to summarize superficially another thinker's work rather than to engage it deeply, and he had in mind both Kierkegaard's and Wittgenstein's own warnings about the difficulties their writings presented to understanding. Holmer's suspicion of easy assimilation might also make anyone writing a book on Holmer take pause. But another strength of Richard Rollefson's book is that he avoids the pitfall of distilling Holmer's thought into a collection of philosophical "results," positions, theories, or paradigms. In the book's title, the phrase "thinking with" invites us rather to think with Holmer in thinking with Kierkegaard and Wittgenstein to achieve not cheaply won "results," but skills in practicing the rigorous critical reflection and strenuous self-examination that together may, as Holmer puts it, "make sense" of our lives.

For all of these reasons, we are indebted to Richard Rollefson, for his book is a reliable and stimulating guide to the thought of Paul L. Holmer, a book that does justice to the depth and complexity of one of the most provocative and interesting philosophical theologians of his generation.

David J. Gouwens
Professor of Theology
Brite Divinity School

Acknowledgments

I WANT TO ACKNOWLEDGE the contribution of my original dissertation advisor, Dr. Timothy Lull. While he was serving as President of Pacific Lutheran Theological Seminary and I was pastoring a nearby church, Tim called me to meet in his office at the seminary. After he inquired about my progress in my doctoral program—knowing quite well that I was long overdue in submitting a topic for my dissertation—I explained that my intent was a definitive work on "The Concept of Truth in Christian Discourse," with a focus on the implications of Kierkegaard's "truth is subjectivity," and the philosophy of the later Wittgenstein for understanding religious language. I had worked up many ever-expanding outlines, but because there was always another book to read for the project, together with time constraints in light of my work as a pastor, I wasn't making much headway. As a fellow graduate of Yale Divinity School, Tim was aware of the significance of Paul Holmer's wedding of the insights of Kierkegaard and Wittgenstein, along with his reappraisal of the traditional concepts of the vices and virtues, which had provided inspiration for several generations of YDS students. It was then that Tim said, "Why don't you write on Paul Holmer's work." I detected in Tim's proposal an echo of Holmer's own voice—in essence—"Cut the intellectual grandiosity and do something that might actually be edifying." Tim was right, and I thank him.

I also thank Dr. David Gouwens, who, as an editor of The Paul L. Holmer Papers, was kind enough to give his time to read and comment on this work.

I am grateful to the people of Shepherd of the Hills Lutheran Church for granting me the time to complete the original dissertation and to F.

Acknowledgments

Bailey Green, for Sabbath time at his house in The Sea Ranch, California, to work on its revision.

Lastly, thanks to my wife, Cyndi, for her love and support.

Introduction

THE PHILOSOPHICAL THEOLOGY OF Paul L. Holmer brings together two fundamental concerns: what Holmer terms, on the one hand, the "logical," and on the other, the "ethico-religious." In dealing with these issues, Holmer's thought parallels that of the two major sources of his own intellectual development: the writings of Søren Kierkegaard and Ludwig Wittgenstein. The intent of this essay is to examine the interplay of these two concerns in the writings of Paul Holmer and to discuss their significance for contemporary Christian theological and ethical reflection. It is the thesis of the pages that follow that Paul Holmer's work offers a unique approach to the fundamental orientation of theological and ethical reflection, and that this approach has significant implications for both the method and the content of theological reflection. In particular, Holmer's explication of theology as "the grammar of faith" proposes an important alternative to predominant contemporary perspectives on the nature and purpose of Christian theology.

Paul Holmer was born November 14, 1916, in Minneapolis, Minnesota. He attended the University of Chicago and University of Minnesota and received his bachelor of arts degree from the latter in 1940. In the same year he began his graduate work in philosophy at Yale University, completing his MA in 1942 and the PhD in 1946. From 1945 through 1948, Dr. Holmer served as an instructor in philosophy, first at Yale and later at the University of Minnesota. Once at Minnesota, Dr. Holmer quickly moved from the rank of assistant to associate professor; he was awarded a full professorship in 1950 and taught at Minnesota until 1960. In that same year, he moved to Yale University, teaching both in the graduate program of religious studies and at the divinity school as Noah Porter Professor of Philosophical Theology. Dr. Holmer retired from Yale in May 1987.

Thinking with Kierkegaard and Wittgenstein

It was in the context of the ascendancy of logical positivism and linguistic analysis that Holmer, as a Kierkegaard scholar, forwarded a distinctive approach for understanding religious language.[1] While at Yale, Holmer
began to note the connections between the thought of Kierkegaard and
Wittgenstein, in such a way that, as Richard Bell observes: "They were both
seen to address the human heart by their careful analysis of concepts that
focused attention on how to understand human subjectivity and how to
see our human affections and emotions as part of human life and culture."[2]

Dr. Holmer has had significant influence on a generation of theologians, ethicists and pastors through his varied books and articles and in
courses on Kierkegaard, Philosophical Theology and Ethics at Yale University and the Yale Divinity School. By bringing together the perspectives of
Kierkegaard and Wittgenstein, in conjunction with a renewed appreciation
of a traditional "morality of the virtues," Holmer has, at the least, indirectly
contributed to the so-called Yale school perspective in theology represented by Hans Frei and George Lindbeck and recent reflection in the field of
Christian ethics on the formation Christian character.[3]

1. Bell, *Grammar of the Heart*. In his introduction to this collection of essays in honor
of Paul Holmer, Richard Bell notes that the University of Minnesota was a center of
logical positivism in the period of Holmer's tenure and work on Kierkegaard. He also
places Holmer's work within the context of the debates between the "verificationist" and
"emotivist" positions represented in such works as A. J. Ayer's *Language, Truth, and Logic*
and Anthony Flew's *Logic and Language*. According to Bell, it was at Yale that Holmer
first began to "wed some of the ideas of Kierkegaard and Wittgenstein," in a way that
suggested new directions for dealing with the "problem" of religious language.

2. Bell, "Culture, Morality and Religious Belief," in *Grammar of the Heart*, xiii–xiv.
Bell continues: "The logic of the 'stages' in Kierkegaard was seen as a way of mapping
human emotions to show their place in our existence, and Wittgenstein's concept of
'grammar' pointed to the interconnection of our language with our life."

3. See Lindbeck, *Nature of Doctrine*, and Frei, *Eclipse of Biblical Narrative*. As the
editors note in their foreword to *Thinking the Faith with Passion: Selected Essays*, vol. 2 of
The Paul L. Holmer Papers, xii: "While many people are aware that Holmer contributed
something to the 'Yale School,' they are unclear concerning exactly what it was; indeed,
Holmer is often mentioned as an important but shadowy figure." Gouwens cites Lindbeck's note in his *The Nature of Doctrine* (14 n. 28): "I am particularly indebted to my
colleague Paul Holmer for his understanding of what is theologically important about
Wittgenstein. Some sense of the lessons he has tried to convey over the years is provided
by his essay 'Wittgenstein and Theology.'" The editors go on to reference Robert Andrew
Cathey's "sympathetic account" of the connection between Holmer and Lindbeck in his
God in Postliberal Perspective, 49–82. For example, in reference to *The Grammar of Faith*,
Cathey argues that "the particular use that Lindbeck makes of the concept of theology
(especially doctrine) as the grammar of faith . . . is basically consistent with interpretations provided by Bell and Holmer" (64). Cathey also disputes William Placher's decision

Holmer's use of Kierkegaard writings and what is sometimes termed "ordinary language" philosophy is oriented toward the lived experience of the Christian faith and its "first-order" discourse of prayer, confession and worship. He challenges his readers to rigorous reflection on the "logic" of ethical and Christian concepts and the "grammar" which governs the ordinary uses of these concepts. Moreover, as a "morphology of the life of Christian belief," Holmer's work has important implications for theological education, the practice of ministry and the life of faith itself. Our purpose here is to examine these notions of "grammar," "logic" and "morphology" and to demonstrate their significance for contemporary theological reflection.

1. Structure of the Essay

The plan of our discussion is first to present a brief sketch of some of the main themes of Holmer's writings and then to move on to a more extended discussion of his interpretation of Kierkegaard's authorship. The central concerns here are Kierkegaard's understanding of the "logic" of the Christian faith and his view of the self and its possibilities as represented by his concept of "spheres" or "stages of existence."

---

in "Revisionist and Postliberal Theologies and the Public Character of Theology" (408 n. 35) not to treat Holmer's work as central to his account of postliberal theology because of Holmer's alleged "move in the direction of Wittgensteinian Fideism." We discuss Holmer's alleged "fideism" in more detail in chapter 4. On the other hand, in his essay "Postliberal Theology," 42, George Hunsinger challenges the very notion of the "Yale School," characterizing it as having "little basis in reality, being largely the invention of theological journalism," and "united more by what it opposes than by any common theological program." He goes on to argue: "One indication that the Yale School is mostly a fiction is that no two lists of who allegedly belongs to it are the same. . . . Does the Yale Shool include Brevard Childs, David Kelsey and Paul Holmer?" While it is not the intent of this essay to resolve the question of Holmer's participation in or influence upon the "Yale School," it does seem clear that Holmer's reflections on the significance of the philosophy of the later Wittgenstein—particularly his reflections on theology as the grammar of faith, the importance of understanding religious language use in the context of a form of life, the distinction between the first-order language of faith and second-order theological reflection and his challenge to foundationalism—influenced George Lindbeck's work in *The Nature of Doctrine*. Another common theme that Holmer shares with Lindbeck and Frei is the primacy of the biblical narrative for theological reflection. However, despite the points of intersection between the two concerns, Holmer's focus on the passion and logic of faith—"the morphology of Christian belief"—is clearly distinct from Lindbeck's promotion of a "cultural-linguistic theory" of religion.

The next topic is Holmer's interpretation and use of the later philosophy of Ludwig Wittgenstein. A central concern here is Wittgenstein's attention to what he terms the "grammar" which governs a mode of discourse and his recognition that only by attending to the human activities or "forms of life" of which the discourse is part can it fully be understood. We will discuss Wittgenstein's notion of "theology as grammar" and the implications of this perspective for understanding the character of religious language and belief. In this context we will also explore Holmer's notion that basic Christian concepts can best be understood as "capacities."

In chapter 3 we turn to Holmer's main constructive work, *The Grammar of Faith* with an eye to his special way of uniting the perspectives of Kierkegaard and Wittgenstein. As Holmer's primary theological proposal, this work offers a significant departure from much contemporary thought on the purpose and method of theology. In this context we will examine both Holmer's critique of contemporary theology and his constructive proposals.

We then turn to a consideration of some of the criticisms of Holmer's philosophical and theological views. Here we will examine and respond to the characterizations of Holmer's work as "fideistic" and "relativistic." The concluding chapter seeks to evaluate the significance of Holmer's theological and ethical perspectives for contemporary theological reflection. We will attempt to make this evaluation by placing our discussion within the context of Holmer's understanding of Christian ethics and his reassessment of traditional concepts of the vices and virtues. Here we will examine his *Making Christian Sense* and *C.S. Lewis: The Shape of His Faith and Thought*. Holmer's emphasis on the role of emotions, passions, and feelings in character formation and ethical behavior is an important feature of his treatment of this topic and serves as a bridge to our earlier discussions of Kierkegaard and Wittgenstein.

It should be noted that our primary purpose is the exposition of Holmer's thought through a close reading of his work. Our intent is to discern the shape and the "how" of his thinking; in this sense, it is to engage his thought and to think with him. For this reason, our treatment does not focus on the development of his thought, nor on his personal history. In following this method we are in keeping with Holmer's own polemic against the assumed primacy of an historical understanding. As Holmer notes in reference to understanding Kierkegaard's works, "Therefore, one is obliged in writing about Kierkegaard to do one of two things: (a), write historical literature about his deeds, his books, the events occasioning either, etc.; or (b), write a critical literature in which one engages the argument, religious and philosophic."[4]

Inasmuch as Holmer shares a subject matter of ethical and religious concern with Kierkegaard which portrays "what any person can in fact become," and that in order to understand in this realm, one must seriously entertain the possibility described, our intent is to follow the latter methodology.

2. Main Themes of Holmer's Thought

Paul Holmer introduces his *Theology and the Scientific Study of Religion*, first published in 1961, in the following way:

> This volume tries to make a clear distinction between the learning about religious matters and the learning (and language) that flows from religious life. It is not enough to say that the Christian faith requires only a way of life or set of attitudes. . . . Again and again, serious and devoted followers of Jesus have looked at language of faith, both the informal and casual expressions on the one side, and the more carefully wrought formulations on the other, as if they were but poor and inappropriate coins in the divine realm.[5]

This distinction between "the learning about religious matters" and "the learning (and language) that flows from religious life" is an early and ongoing theme in Holmer's writings. Holmer also puts this distinction in terms of the contrast between a language "about," and a language "of," faith. This distinction has both formal "grammatical/logical" implications and material consequences for Holmer. As he goes on to state:

> Certainly it is true that religious faith is also a matter of passion, of attitude, and of obedience. Lately though . . . there are some who say that religious language is only emotive, if not completely

4. Holmer, "On Understanding Kierkegaard," 44. Holmer goes on to note: "In the first instance there is no promise of a systematic consequence unless a metaphysics of learning obtains (and then Kierkegaard is wrong); in the second instance one writes not about the man and his books as much as one translates his language and thoughts into one's own." The balance of this article is an argument against assuming that historical study is the key to understanding Kierkegaard's—or any author's—writings. In his *C. S. Lewis*, Holmer notes this same argument in Lewis' *An Experiment in Criticism* and makes the same case in reference to understanding Lewis' writings.

5. Holmer, *Theology and the Scientific Study of Religion*, 9.

> meaningless. It then becomes tempting to retire altogether the doctrinal and time-honored language behind as an artifact of an earlier day. But, in this very breach, religious scholarship has assumed a promising role. . . It now becomes tempting—for the learned and sophisticated—to let these new scientific methods, these contemporary disciplined ways of making old things speak, their furbished inquiries into Scripture, ideas, God, and church, furnish the new "grundlich" stuff of religious affirmation. It will be here argued that this is an egregious error.[6]

What Holmer terms an "egregious error—or better, a number of errors— provides the problematic that the whole of his work seeks to address and the context in which his polemic occurs. As he goes on to state in the introduction to this work: "Within a variety of studies it becomes increasingly clear that there is indeed a language of faith, different in kind and scope from both the everyday patois and the language of scientific study."[7]

The question of the place of "scientific study" and language "about" religion, as contrasted to the language "of faith," is a central issue in all of Holmer's philosophical and ethical work. The issue at stake is the place and role of formal or systematic reflection as compared to the actual language and practice of the life of faith. Where the former properly addresses the concerns of intellectual satisfaction and the desire for objective knowledge, the latter answers the need for "the consolation of an abiding conviction." As we will see, the "learning and language about religious things" and the "learning and language of the religious life" represent for Holmer two distinct approaches; understanding how they differ and the proper place of each is essential to theological and ethical reflection. Indeed, as we have noted, how these two concerns differ not only informs the method of theological reflection but is a topic for this reflection as well. And as Holmer sees it, the failure to recognize the distinction between the two is a confusion which not only affects formal or "scientific" theological reflection but the life of faith as well. To put the matter in more concrete terms—as Holmer himself always does—"learning about the things of faith is not the same as learning to be faithful."[8]

Because of his perception of this problem and the difficulty of exorcising its pervasive influence, a second characteristic of much of Holmer's

6. Ibid., 10.

7. Ibid.

8. Ibid., 12.

writing is its polemical tone. Such a tone is, of course, in keeping with both the writings of Kierkegaard and those of Wittgenstein. Where a "monstrous illusion" is being perpetuated, where the fly resists being "shewn" the way out of the bottle, a strong and consistent therapy is required. Persons rarely wish to be shown that they are mistaken and when the mistake being pointed out involves one's basic conceptual orientation polemical rhetoric is perhaps unavoidable. And yet, the argumentative character of Holmer's work has meant that it is sometimes misunderstood or even dismissed. Some have even suggested that there is a "reactionary" or "anti-intellectual" character to Holmer's writing. It must be said, however, that those whose thought Holmer criticizes most vehemently are well served by what is often a superficial rejection of his work. It is part of the burden of this essay to demonstrate that such treatment of Holmer's thought is undeserved.

Another way of stating the distinction between a language "about faith" and the language "of faith" is to distinguish between simple intellectual curiosity and what Holmer terms a "religious interest." While a religious interest may be served by intellectual efforts, Holmer assumes Pascal's perspective, translating the latter's aphorism: "The science of physical things will not, in time of affliction, make up for the lack of moral practice."[9] In Holmer's view, knowledge itself will not solve intimate ethical dilemmas, continuing emotional wants or attitudes. A language about faith only describes various possibilities; it is not, however, until one encounters these possibilities in one's own experience and is challenged to a decision for or against a religious way of life that real understanding is achieved. It is Kierkegaard's view of the peculiar logic of Christian belief, along with Wittgenstein's observation that particular uses of language belong to a "form of life" and cannot be understood apart from it, that underscore Holmer's position on this issue.

It is not, however, knowledge itself that is at issue for Holmer, but rather a mistaken belief that accompanies learning about things religious. It is the assumption that knowledge about religion replaces the need and even the legitimacy of religious ways of thinking, talking and acting. In this view religious language, the language "of" faith, must be translated into another more general and abstract conceptuality if it is to be meaningful. It is the need for such "translation" that Holmer rejects.

---

9. Pascal, *Pensees*, no. 105, quoted in Holmer, *Theology and the Scientific Study of Religion*, 14.

Another related theme is the place of doubt within religious language and reflection. Because intellectual doubt about specific doctrines and formulations of belief are a part of the life of faith, in the quest for intellectual certainty, there is an inevitable temptation to exchange the interest in being a Christian for an interest about Christian things where "the passion for the new life in Christ, the genuine root of need and quest [is] diverted into an enthusiasm for scholarship about Christ, about Christian ideas . . ."[10] In this way, the focus of one's concern changes from passionate interest in a way of life to a more limited concern with intellectual certainty. The problem, in Holmer's view, is that in the ethical and religious realms learning about morals is not the same thing as learning to be moral, learning about faith does not necessarily lead one to be faithful.

Holmer argues instead that theology is properly "a language and learning expressive of pathos, enthusiasm and even passion."[11] This concern with the "passion" and "pathos" of the language of faith marks another theme in Holmer's writings. Like Kierkegaard, Holmer is concerned with the passion and commitment which are part of the "logic" of religious faith and language. The language of faith is not, nor should it be, detached or disinterested, and it is this language which theology describes.

It is for this reason that Holmer argues for the autonomy of ethics and faith. Neither faith nor ethics are the consequences of knowledge. Holmer opposes Kant's "heteronomy" wherein religion and moral action are conceived to be subject to laws or principles external to themselves. And this is the case because theological convictions are not hypotheses that are shown to be probable or improbable on the basis of evidence. This, too, is a theme of Holmer's writing, and as we shall note, a perspective in keeping with the philosophical analysis of Ludwig Wittgenstein.

Another theme related to concerns taken up by both Kierkegaard and Wittgenstein is the relation between theological and philosophical reflection. Both Kierkegaard and Wittgenstein were critical of a view wherein the relation of philosophy to theology is conceived in terms of the former discovering or providing the latter with a ground or foundation. Philosophy, in this view, deals with what is seen to be the proper evidence or "the reasons" for belief, whereas what believers themselves give as "reasons" for their beliefs are necessarily discounted.

10. Ibid., 16.
11. Ibid., 18.

As Holmer came to see, in their distinctive ways, both Kierkegaard and Wittgenstein argue for the legitimacy of religious language and belief apart from philosophical foundations. Indeed the search for such foundations is itself called into question given the distinctive logic of religious beliefs. In Wittgenstein's view, religious language and beliefs have their grounding in a religious form or way of life. The proper role of philosophical analysis in reference to belief is to examine the distinctive character and logic of religious language as it occurs within the life of faith. The meaningfulness of religious utterances is therefore seen in the role they play in the lives of believers. It is this connection of belief and practice, language and life, to which Holmer draws our attention in the pages that follow. For as Holmer himself argues, what it means properly to reflect on ethical and religious concerns—and what it means to be an ethical or religious person—is to bring together words and practices, language and life, in such a way that they form a human life.

I believe it can be argued—and I intend to demonstrate—that the contribution of Paul L. Holmer's thought is of such significance that it deserves a wider readership and greater recognition. It is to benefit the work of theological reflection and, indeed, the very life of faith, that this examination of Holmer's writings is presented.

1

Kierkegaard and the Morphology of the Self

1. Introduction

IT IS IN LIGHT of his reading, interpretation and use of the writings of Søren Kierkegaard that Paul Holmer is perhaps best known. Holmer's doctoral work focused on Kierkegaard and he has written extensively on various issues within Kierkegaard's authorship. Throughout his teaching career at Yale University, Holmer's "Readings in Kierkegaard" was consistently among the most provocative and popular courses.[1]

This early interest in Kierkegaard is at the basis of Holmer's own blending of broadly philosophical and specifically Christian concerns. One of the chief issues addressed in Holmer's philosophy and theology has been the development of the self and the role of self-understanding in ethical and religious life. This concern with charting human subjectivity and showing the "logic" of the self in the context of ethical and religious formation is clearly informed by Holmer's reading of Kierkegaard. In this sense it may be said that the central question of what it is to be a self and the relation of this question to ethical and logical concerns forms the context for both Søren Kierkegaard's and Paul Holmer's philosophical and religious writings. And

1. In their recent compilation of Holmer's writings on Kierkegaard, David Gouwens and Lee Barrett III have reconstructed Holmer's unpublished book-length draft manuscript on Kierkegaard under the title, *On Kierkegaard and the Truth*. In addition, several previously unpublished manuscripts on Kierkegaard are included in a second volume of Holmer's papers, *Thinking the Faith with Passion*. The substance of this essay was written prior to the publication of these volumes; citations have been updated with reference to these collections where possible.

it is in light of his early and continuing reflection on Kierkegaard's writings in conjunction with those of Ludwig Wittgenstein that Holmer develops and pursues a vision of philosophical theology as an examination of the grammar and logic of ethical and specifically Christian language and life.[2] The concept of "subjectivity" is central here and, as we shall show, has reference to both the individual human self as "subject," the personal involvement involved in the formation of self identity, and the particular logic and appropriation of ethical and religious truth. The fact that in Kierkegaard's literature becoming an authentic self is directly connected to the "truth as subjectivity" which the Christian faith represents, means, I believe, that the whole of Kierkegaard's literary output may be understood as an extended reflection on the "truth" of the Christian faith, on the mode of apprehending and communicating this truth and on the form of existence both enabled and demanded by one who would live this truth.

As the primary concerns in much of Holmer's writings, it is in conversation with Kierkegaard that Holmer's own perspectives on these issues were developed and refined. In this chapter we will explore the correlation of what it is to be a self—and more specifically, an "authentic self"—as interpreted by Holmer, in light of Kierkegaard's thesis that in reference to Christianity, "truth is subjectivity."

2. On Reading Kierkegaard

As presented by Holmer, Kierkegaard's writings are best understood as a whole—as an "authorship"—to use Kierkegaard's own term. This authorship includes both the pseudonymous writings and those to which Kierkegaard's own name is directly attributed. As Holmer observes, taken as a whole, it is a difficult range of literature to easily summarize:

> For that literature includes both objective and sheer aesthetic creations and intimate self-expression; it is both argument and

2. As Gouwens and Barrett III note in reviewing drafts of Holmer's manuscript on Kierkegaard: "As the drafts evolved, the influence of Ludwig Wittgenstein became more evident. In Wittgenstein Holmer discerned an illuminating parallel to Kierkegaard's theme that the way of appropriating and using a concept is constitutive of its meaning. Wittgenstein's attention to the particularities of context and purpose seemed to him to clarify Kierkegaard's insistence that the right context of pathos must be present for religious and moral discourse to be meaningful. The concept 'God' cannot be grasped without imagining the purpose of praising, confessing, and exhorting in which the concept 'God' is embedded" (Holmer, *On Kierkegaard and the Truth*, xix).

logically precise polemic and passional effusion; it is both the first-person singular and the third-person singular modes; it is both analytic description of forms of life and an unashamed avowal of the Christian faith. The very multiplicity of the literature and the kind of responses it requires is how it tests the reader, especially the academic reader, so severely.[3]

Given Kierkegaard's unique literature and his concern with the "existence" of the thinker, he has often been critiqued as an "irrationalist" or "subjectivist." Part of the burden of Holmer's interpretation of Kierkegaard is to demonstrate that this is simply not the case. Holmer contends that Kierkegaard is neither a subjectivist nor an "existentialist" in the popular sense of the term. He writes: "It is tempting to place his numerous diatribes, his remarks on absurdity, his notion that the reality cannot be a system, his stress on subjectivity, into familiar categories and thereby lump him with other anti-intellectualists, sophisticated and vulgar. But this will not finally be a successful way of understanding Kierkegaard."[4]

In the first place this means for Holmer that Kierkegaard's writings are not simply a personal expression and the craft he practices is neither subjective, self-disclosing, emotive nor directly passional.[5] One implication of this perspective, in contrast to many interpretations of Kierkegaard's literature, is that it is not to be understood as a projection of issues and events within Kierkegaard's personal history. Suggestive of both Kierkegaard's and his own polemic against "academics," Holmer observes that the intellectuals will "do almost anything but engage his literature and its respective demands and will instead look for clues elsewhere, particularly in his life and particularly in his journal."[6] But the historical facts of his life, however much we may know about them, do not for Holmer constitute "the meaning" of Kierkegaard's writings. In the same way, although Kierkegaard wrote a great deal about his own books in the *Postscript, The Point of View for My Work as an Author,* and his *Papier,* Holmer argues that he "never quite gratified the deceit . . . that an author is the best interpreter of his own words."[7]

3. Holmer, "Post-Kierkegaardian Remarks About Being a Person," 5.

4. Ibid., 4.

5. Holmer, "About Being a Person," 54. We will continue to note the titles of individual essays collected in this volume.

6. Holmer, "Post-Kierkegaardian Remarks," 4.

7. Ibid., 2. As Holmer notes in "Understanding Kierkegaard," 40: "Every author imposes limitations upon his readers. . . . Kierkegaard is no exception to this rule. But what

Secondly, in all his treatments of Kierkegaard's writings, Holmer is especially conscious of the danger of misrepresenting Kierkegaard's thought by pretending to have gotten at what some have called the "essence" or the "secret" of this literature. He notes:

> It is very difficult not to be a sophist and sell other people's ideas. Furthermore, it is altogether too easy to betray another thinker's ideas, especially if they are radical and new in form, by using the conventional rubrics and quasi-scholarly devices of the intellectual establishment. Not only is it morally wrong to use other's lives and thoughts for giving honor to oneself, for playing academic games, and for getting to hard-earned results by cheap secondhand means, but it is sometimes plainly deceptive to do a scholarly precis.[8]

In the same way Holmer goes on to observe that almost every interpreter who summarizes Kierkegaard's thought in order to state what he was "really doing" is prone to betraying the aim of his philosophy. Holmer notes that Kierkegaard himself predicted that his thought would be taken over by academics, misinterpreted and used to promulgate a new "school" of thought: "In Kierkegaard's case the academic world has had to invent another category, namely, existentialism. Here he becomes an advocate by induction, a progenitor by anticipation, of a school of thought, a metaphysician and a system-builder, despite himself."[9] This kind of "assimilation" of his literature is, according to Holmer, a dismissal of the real implications of Kierkegaard's thought, for it treats it merely as an additional "theory" and leaves out of the equation the essential aspect of personal appropriation. Echoing Kierkegaard's own polemic Holmer notes: "His notion is that his literature is primarily a way of tearing away the illusions and defenses, the silly methodologies and funded cultural responses that keep us from responding in a primitive and clear way to actual existence. His point is not to erect one more theory, one more artifice, one more permutation of reflection, by which we are supposed to come to terms with reality. What he is about is an attack upon these and related notions."[10]

---

distinguishes him is that he noted such matters and frequently commented upon them, referring repeatedly to his own writings. Of course, no author's words are obligatory for the reader, not even, strangely enough, if they happen to be true. Indicative sentences, even if true, are not imperatives."

8. Holmer, "Kierkegaard and Philosophy," 4.

9. Holmer, "Post-Kierkegaardian Remarks," 8.

10. Ibid., 5.

Where most interpreters of Kierkegaard's writings have gone wrong, in Holmer's view, is in assuming that issues of moral and religious life are somehow a matter of cognitive and intellectual problems and dependent upon their resolution as such. Indeed, this is a primary critique that Kierkegaard directs against the philosophy of his own time. In contrast, Holmer recognizes Kierkegaard's repeated critique that we have forgotten "what it means to exist"; rather than trying to think our personal existence in the same way that we think everything else, Kierkegaard shows us "a radical difference." In Holmer's terms, Kierkegaard's writings "are a discipline and a way, not another theory."[11] For this reason a fundamental theme in Holmer's reading of Kierkegaard is his attempt to do justice to both the content and the intent of Kierkegaard's literature. And for this same reason, Holmer's treatment of themes within Kierkegaard's literature are always prefaced by an urgent request that readers themselves first look at Kierkegaard's literature and use Holmer's own reflections only as a secondary aid in this reading.

Insofar as Holmer views Kierkegaard's writings as dealing with the issue of subjectivity without their being merely subjective, he contends that Kierkegaard "writes an entire literature whose spirit is outside the main strands of western theological and philosophical thought":

> Against the loose view articulated by both philosophers and poets, Kierkegaard did not believe that subjectivity and interests were unintelligible and formless. There is a kind of "logos" and order and structure that permits description and makes poetry and creative literature expressive of more than the idiosyncratic self. Language describing subjectivity can be communicated because there are actual inter-subjective elements.[12]

Revealing his own polemical perspective on the issue, Holmer states that "the bugaboo for so many academic people is always subjectivity," and he goes on to note that "what is forgotten in this context, bracketed by the cryptic notion that either one must be objective or otherwise subjectivity runs riot, is that such dichotomous reasoning is misleading on a whole range of issue."[13] In contrast to such views, it is Holmer's contention that the whole of Kierkegaard's authorship demonstrates the order and logic of the subjective dimension of life: "He offers his array of authors and their

11. Ibid., 8.

12. Holmer, "Kierkegaard and Religious Propositions," 135–36.

13. Holmer, "About Being a Person," 55–56.

literature to show that 'emotions' and 'passions,' those factors which have been scorned as subjective and mad, wanton and rule-less, can be and are ruled and ingredient in aesthetic, moral and religious concepts."[14]

This is a clue to the meaning of "subjectivity" within Kierkegaard's literature and in Holmer's own philosophical and theological reflections. Kierkegaard call his works *Fear and Trembling, Sickness Unto Death, The Concept of Dread, The Concept of Irony,* and *Repetition,* "psychological studies." Kierkegaard is clearly not doing psychology in the contemporary sense of seeking the causal explanations of human behavior or the structures of psychological happenings; rather, as Holmer puts it, Kierkegaard "is more properly described as doing philosophical psychology, for he is everywhere detecting, isolating, then describing . . . to show us that feelings have inherent order, structure, even systems, that valuations fall into groups and types and are not random."[15] Thus, a major theme in Holmer's interpretation is that Kierkegaard's work repudiates the notion that reason and passion are mutually exclusive of one another and instead supplies "a kind of map, a logical one, of the emotional cosmos."[16] As we shall see, it is an analogous kind of mapping, "the morphology of the life of Christian belief," that Holmer proposes in his *The Grammar of Faith.*

In addition to these concerns, Holmer notes that within the overall project of Kierkegaard's literature those works with his own name attached are often overlooked. But in Holmer's understanding of Kierkegaard's literature, these writings are essential to Kierkegaard's larger intent and help in interpreting and understanding the rest of the literature. For example, in his introduction to a selection of Kierkegaard's *Edifying Discourses,* Holmer makes a simple observation that these essays are "calculated to bring the reader . . . into conversation about religious and Christian concerns."[17] He goes on to describe Kierkegaard's orientation in the *Discourses* by observing that he seeks to address the universally human in each of us; however, "against those who have identified the universally human with rationality or as aesthetic sensibility or as an endowment of natural rights, Kierkegaard insists that the truly universal and distinctively human factor lies in subjectivity and inwardness."[18]

14. Holmer, "Kierkegaard and Philosophy," 13.

15. Ibid., 17.

16. Ibid., 14.

17. Holmer, "Introduction," in Kierkegaard, *Edifying Discourses,* vii.

18. Ibid.

As Holmer understands them, the *Discourses* are attempts "to stimulate and also to discipline our feelings, wishes and hopes. Kierkegaard does not try to convey results as much as to elicit in his reader a self-activity and process of appropriation."[19] As we will show, Holmer shares the conviction he attributes to Kierkegaard that everyone "is potentially a being of spirit," and that "the awakening of inwardness is the beginning of the relationship to God."[20]

Holmer has been almost alone in recognizing the significance of Kierkegaard's *Discourses* and understanding their place within his larger literary project. As he writes: "No one can understand Kierkegaard's authorship unless he also fathoms these discourse, for here the litmus test of Kierkegaard's thought and conviction must finally be made."[21] According to Holmer, in contrast to his philosophical works, it is the very simplicity of the *Discourses* that is the key to their significance within Kierkegaard's literature as a whole:

> His philosophy succeeded in taking him out of the speculative, the poetic, and the aristocratic, back to the simple and the edifying. For this reason, Kierkegaard could insist that the religious discourses, slight as they appear in comparison, nevertheless enable the reader to interpret the more imposing philosophic works. Just as he argued that philosophy could not really distill the gist of religion anyway, so to, Kierkegaard's own literature is contrived so ironically that the simple discourses become more crucial and important to any reader who understands them than the profound and difficult philosophic pieces.[22]

Holmer observes that the category of "religious or edifying discourse" is a precise one for Kierkegaard. Kierkegaard called these writings discourses rather than sermons because they take as their point of departure a "universally human" rather than specifically Christian perspective. It is the human situation, and the ethical categories of immanence which are evidenced in them rather than the authority of Scripture or doctrine. Furthermore, according to Holmer, the discourses are "exploratory" in a philosophic manner: the aim is "to tease out of the human being's ethical

19. Ibid.
20. Ibid.
21. Ibid., xi.
22. Ibid., xii.

life those considerations which are upbuilding and regenerative."[23] In this manner, the edifying discourses, as addresses to the human situation, are, without being specifically Christian in orientation, preparatory to the Christian faith. As Holmer notes:

> They are an illustration of the fact the edifying is a wider category than the Christian. Kierkegaard insists that Christianity is edifying. By this he means that it too builds up or constitutes human beings as ethical subjects. Christian faith does have moral consequences: it makes an empirical difference in the lives of men. From such facts, however, it does not follow that every edifying truth is Christian.[24]

Speaking more directly, and yet without the authority of specifically Christian categories, Kierkegaard seeks to bring the subjectivity of the reader to the point of eligibility for Christian inwardness and concern.

It is in this way that the *Edifying Discourses* have their place within the larger corpus of Kierkegaard's writings. For, according to Holmer, "Kierkegaard's constant and life-long wish, to which his entire authorship gives expression, was to create a new and rich subjectivity in himself and his readers."[25] For this reason, then, Holmer can characterize the *Discourses* as "the goal of the literature" as a whole. Although like the pseudonymous writings these addresses do not seek to convey results, they do, according to Holmer, "aim to elicit that specific kind of existing, that mode of subjectivity and inwardness, which is the truth for every reader."[26]

For these reasons, I believe it may be said that Holmer comes to understand the whole of Kierkegaard's authorship in light of these works. This perspective informs Holmer's overall interpretation of Kierkegaard's literature and colors his reading of even the pseudonymous literature. This is not to impose an interpretation on Kierkegaard's larger authorship, nor does it mean that each of the pseudonymous works cannot be read or understood on its own terms.[27] Holmer is convinced, however, that the overarching

23. Ibid., xiv.

24. Ibid.

25. Ibid., xviii.

26. Ibid.

27. In recognition of the independent content and meaningfulness of each of Kierkegaard's works, Holmer notes in "Kierkegaard and Philosophy," 16–17, that "every one of his books in a fashion provides an analysis of a specific concept, invariably by reference to the histories, moods and passions of people. Whenever there are practices, habits, established ways, there he finds a concept to spring forth. These detailed analyses,

concern and ongoing purpose throughout his literature is best understood in reference to Kierkegaard's avowed intent of seeking to become a Christian himself. As Holmer observes: "Kierkegaard was seeking to be a Christian. Christianity was the truth for every man because it alone described that kind of subjectivity which is sufficient to the human quest. It is toward such an end that his discourses lead his readers."[28]

What Holmer discerns via the unique character of Kierkegaard's literature, then, is an understanding and meaning which only the reader can engender but which is not, for that cause, subjective, private or idiosyncratic. The descriptive rendering of the "logic of the self" is one of Holmer's chief concerns in his interpretation of Kierkegaard and, at the same time, his own reflection on this logic is one of Holmer's primary contributions to contemporary philosophical theology. We shall now turn to some of the significant themes in Kierkegaard's "philosophical psychology" as Holmer's treatment of them serves to demonstrate his understanding and use of Kierkegaard's writings.

3. Consciousness: Knowledge "About" versus Knowledge "Of"

In one presentation of Kierkegaard's "stages or spheres of existence" Holmer speaks about the aesthetic, the ethical and the religious stages as ideal or generalized modes of "consciousness" on the part of individuals. In this view, the stages are "like self-projections, like organized ways of responding to existence itself."[29] "Being conscious" in the most immediate sense of Holmer's usage refers to the ways "that people typically learn to see, hear and think in an 'about mood.'"[30] As persons begin to learn "about" something and acquire knowledge, according to Holmer, they begin to "intend" the world and make statements about it; the result is that "knowing the world is done in social ways, in language that must be public and for purposes that are recognizable and by and large stateable."[31] "Transivity" is the term Holmer uses for this characteristic of consciousness, which he describes as "the

of differences between moral 'guilt,' and 'sin,' 'doubt' concerning truth claims, and 'doubt' concerning oneself, and many more, make each book useful in itself, quite apart from the purposes it might play in the literature as a totality."

28. Holmer, "Introduction," in Kierkegaard, *Edifying Discourses*, xviii.

29. Holmer, "Post-Kierkegaardian Remarks," 6.

30. Holmer, "About Being a Person," 58.

31. Ibid.

intentional and referential thrust that is given everything psychological, so that it becomes the medium for 'aboutness.'"[32] As Holmer notes elsewhere: "Our subjectivity is in fact formed, molded and adapted to the way that the world obtrudes upon us and the managerial pressures that each of us bring to bear upon our activities."[33]

In Holmer's view Kierkegaard is clearly not an anti-intellectualist or skeptic in the sense that he disparages our ability to know the world through concepts; nor does Kierkegaard claim that we know only ideas and not the world itself. Rather, as human beings become conscious "of" and attentive "to" the world around them, they are distinguished from animals "by acquiring all that allows them to intend the world in its very rich and ever-changing manifold."[34] This kind of consciousness, however, is only the preliminary stage in what it means to be a self according to Holmer. For consciousness is not yet fully developed when an individual learns to intend the world in cognitive ways; as Holmer puts it, a person's ability to see, to hear, and to know the world, even if one should become a virtuoso of science and scholarship, "is not to become all that a human being should and can be."[35]

According to Holmer there is another and deeper dimension or form to consciousness than merely intending in the sense of cognitive knowledge "about" the world. Consciousness is altered when one makes of oneself an object of attention and it is this second dimension which specifically constitutes a human being as a "self." For in addition to knowledge "about" the world there is the possibility of a knowledge "of" the self. It is this kind of knowledge, and the interests which give rise to it, that is the context of ethical and religious understanding. As Holmer puts it, "we can also begin to adapt in conscious ways and to constitute ourselves, by choice, decisions purposing, plans, wishes and more."[36]

The achievement of this kind of reflective knowledge of the self is not, however, inevitable. It is here that Kierkegaard's polemic against objective knowledge finds its place. As Holmer interprets Kierkegaard, there is a "diseased and sickened consciousness" which grows directly alongside the acquisition of knowledge about the world. The issue at stake in Kierkegaard's

32. Ibid.
33. Holmer, "Post-Kierkegaardian Remarks," 6.
34. Holmer, "About Being a Person," 58.
35. Holmer, "Post-Kierkegaardian Remarks," 11.
36. Ibid., 6.

polemic is that the accumulation of factual knowledge about the world gives rise to the assumption that the same path of knowledge is the way to personal knowledge of one's self. We come to think that growth in knowledge is quantifiable and that problems of self-understanding can be resolved simply by the acquisition of more factual or objective knowledge. But to think that growth in objective knowledge results at the same time in a growth of consciousness "of" the self is to misconstrue the essential nature of what it is to be, or better, "to become" a self.

According to Holmer, a similar cognitive mistake is made by the dominant strain of Western philosophy when it operates under the assumption that the self needs to be subsumed as part of a whole or system that must first be known: "Our daily life requires long-term wants, even passions and deep feeling. It is Kierkegaard's notion that understanding ourselves and our tasks already supposes highly qualified interests. Hence he attacks the academic convention that most of us illustrate that first we must have the understanding (the theory) and this disinterestedly; and secondly, and subsequently, that the emotions and pathos will then flow as a matter of course."[37]

It is here that the formal logical issues at stake in the conflict between subjectivity and objectivity are seen. For it is not merely an issue of failing to accumulate sufficient objective knowledge of oneself that is at stake, but that real knowledge of the self is concerned, "subjective" knowledge, and this necessarily so: "It would be impossible in the strongest logical sense of 'impossible,'" writes Holmer, "to know clearly and acutely what one was and not, therewith, to be passionately involved. That is why self-consciousness is a different kind of transitivity. It is not knowledge simply turned inward."[38]

For both Kierkegaard and Holmer, the range of issues where this mistaken move is of chief concern is in the area of ethical and religious interest. For it is part of the very "logic" of discourse in these realms that their context is one of feeling, purposing, and hoping, and when these issues are abstracted from the affective life of an individual and treated in an "objective" manner, they are thereby truncated and falsified. In Holmer's view, it is Kierkegaard's intention throughout his literature to call his reader's attention to this fact by dealing with these issues only in the context of the description of a way of life.

Once again, because the task of becoming a self is a reflective activity, "nurtured by choosing, willing, judging and thinking," according to

37. Ibid., 12.
38. Holmer, "About Being a Person," 63.

Holmer, it is necessarily passionate, concerned thinking, "not disinterested, not theoretical, and not objective (in the customary uses of that term); however, it is not "subjective" in the sense that it is merely "wishful think-ing," for "it is about something," and therefore "objective after all, meaning then that it 'refers' and is not idle."[39]

In this sense, then, knowledge of self is independent of one's cogni-tive grasp of the world. As Holmer puts it, for Kierkegaard there are two distinct "dialectical streams" that meet in the individual but do not merge into one: "These two kind of dialectic, one existential, the other cognitive, are not internally related so that persons can be religious, aesthetic or ethi-cal and still have the same science or scholarship."[40] Holmer goes on to note that "intellectuals typically fall into the pattern of thinking that forms of living, ways of being persons, ways of being aesthetic (even in the artistic sense), moral and even religious, are somehow a matter of cognitive and intellectual problems and dependent upon their resolution."[41] In order to address these issues, according to Holmer, Kierkegaard had to invent a genre outside the mainstream of Western philosophical and theological tradition, to show that "becoming aesthetes, or moral, or religious persons, is a more primitive and fundamental matter than is being a knower."[42] And the reason for this last point is that what these "forms of life" depict is our need to become persons and to constitute ourselves as individuals. Another way to say it is that asking questions, posing problems, even becoming ob-jective, is, in the end, "something that subjects do."[43] It is in the context of this critique that Kierkegaard's charting of human "subjectivity" in terms of "spheres of existence" finds its place.

4. The Conflict of Consciousness

As Holmer understands it, a common, perhaps universal human experience is that of finding that one's immediate wants and wishes are at odds with one

---

39. Holmer, "Post-Kierkegaardian Remarks," 15. In this sense, according to Holmer, there is an understanding of "objective" which does not exclude interest and concern, and it is this meaning of "objective" which is properly operative in the area of ethical and religious concern.

40. Holmer, "About Being a Person," 64.

41 Holmer, "Post-Kierkegaardian Remarks," 5–6.

42. Ibid., 6.

43. Ibid.

another. In such situations, there is a division within a person that no amount of additional objective knowledge can overcome. For the issue here is not that of objective knowledge of options, but knowledge of who one is and what one most deeply desires. If appropriately reflected upon, the pursuit of purely objective knowledge in this realm can even serve to increase this awareness; for when it is recognized that the conflict at issue lies not in the realm of cognitive knowledge but in the self's relation to itself, movement is made possible. The danger, however, is that this conflict may simply be labeled a temporary aberration rather that being seen for what it is, namely, a fundamental issue within human existence. Unless this conflict is recognized and directly confronted and a capacity for a new kind of understanding developed, no real growth in self-understanding can occur.

As Holmer presents it, the purpose of Kierkegaard's writings—in particular the pseudonymous writings—is to summarize this conflict and the potential of movement and growth in self-understanding within the generalized categories of the aesthetic, the ethical, and the religious spheres of existence as these present the fundamental ways that human personality is formed. Holmer further argues that Kierkegaard's writings depicting the various spheres or stages of existence show this conflict from within particular modes of self-understanding or forms of life precisely to induce the "crisis of consciousness" that is necessary for the movement from one sphere of self-understanding to another. It is for this reason that

> he shows us individuals, a rich variety of them, with all kinds of self-interest, enthusiasm, despair and all the rest. The literature, then, is not a theory so much as it is a locus for forms of life and kinds of subjectivity. . . . It is calculated both to show something (show it, not say it) and also to create unrest and activity within the reader. It tries to communicate so that we become something different, realize new capacities, and activate our own personalities.[44]

In light of this, Kierkegaard's pseudonymous works are properly understood, according to Holmer, "to fit together and articulate a plan, even a kind of logic that is morphological and also the means of effecting a teaching aim."[45] And in this sense the pseudonymous literature is no mere artistic deception but instead a pedagogical tool to aid readers in their own movement toward greater self understanding.

44. Ibid., 9.
45. Ibid., 10.

As we have suggested, the kind of consciousness that is required for the development of the self is consciousness of oneself: "Consciousness becomes something quite different when a person learns to make himself an object of attention, concern and even knowledge. This is to intend and to purpose oneself: and this kind of transitivity is for Kierkegaard the hallmark of spirituality. This is why he says in *The Sickness Unto Death* that Christian heroism consists principally in venturing to be oneself.[46]

In contrast to this intentional knowledge of the self is a kind of "spiritlessness" which Kierkegaard outlines in *The Present Age, The Sickness Unto Death*, and elsewhere. In the context of an age in which "men have forgotten what it means to exist and what inwardness signifies," Kierkegaard's entire authorship is concerned with showing that to become a self is to take up the task of inwardness and that this task "requires that interests and enthusiasm, concern and passion, be developed for the quality of one's own life."[47] As we have emphasized, it is this capacity, this combination of passion and interest, that is essential to understanding in the realm of ethics and religion as the realm of knowledge "of" the self. As a kind of therapy for this situation, Kierkegaard's writings reflect the general possibilities for human self-understanding, not to provide objective information, but to encourage subjective self-understanding. For ultimately in Kierkegaard's perspective, there is no simple mediation from one sphere to another, but rather a "breach of consciousness" that requires a new "capacity" for self-understanding.[48]

46. Holmer "About Being a Person," 61.

47. Ibid.

48. In reference to Kierkegaard's requirement of the development of a "capacity" to understand, Holmer observes in his "About Being a Person," 57: "And capacity here does suggest that one must have some room in his life (perhaps as the expression *rummelighted* suggests) . . ." The term "capacity" is an important one for Holmer and suggests both the difference between ways of knowing and the way in which a particular stage of existence is a distinctive form of life which involves the use of particular concepts. As we will note at a later point, in Holmer's view, concepts may themselves be understood as such "capacities."

In the case of the first notion of different ways of knowing, where the acquisition of objective knowledge may be described as a "knowing that" occurring in the "about" mood, the kind of knowledge necessary for self-understanding concerns a knowledge "of" which is more akin to "knowing how" to do something. While we will further explore Holmer's use of these terms in our chapter on *The Grammar of Faith*, we may reiterate at this point that the "learning how" appropriate to ethical and religious understanding is the personal appropriation of a way of life rather than the gaining of information.

One place that Holmer suggests this idea of "capacity" is in his treatment of the concept

5. The Concept of the Self and the Spheres of Existence

As Kierkegaard states in a problematic passage from *The Sickness Unto Death*: "The self is a relation which relates itself to its own self, or it is that in the relation (which accounts for it) that the relation relates itself to its own

---

of "understanding" (note his "History and Understanding," 114–18). "Understanding," as Holmer views it, is akin to "having taste" in the sense that you cannot provide taste only by giving other people your judgments unless "you were also able somehow to engender the qualities of life and thought that 'being tasteful,' or 'having taste' requires." In this sense, "to understand" means to have the capacities of appreciation and discernment, which cannot be provided merely by a definition or explanation. Holmer argues that, in a similar sense, concepts such as "God" or "love" are not simply names to be understood by means of a definition, and he sees in Kierkegaard's conceptual studies a more significant treatment of what it means "to understand" in these cases. For example, Kierkegaard writes in his *The Concept of Dread*, 131: "The man who really loves can hardly find pleasure and satisfaction, not to say increase of love, by busying himself with a definition of what love really is. The man who lives in daily and yet solemn familiarity with the thought that there is a God could hardly wish to spoil this thought for himself or see it spoiled by piecing together a definition of what God is."

As Kierkegaard's treatments suggest, the full meaning of these concepts cannot be understood if they are abstracted from the concrete contexts in which they are used. To remove the concepts from the working context in which they are most commonly employed and to put them instead in the artificial one of "definition" is, in fact, to misunderstand them. In these cases, the meaning of the words is bound up with a complicated mode of life in such a way that the meaning cannot simply be "said." Rather, "to understand" in these cases requires not a definition of words but a well-developed personality, a "spirited and well-articulated person." What Kierkegaard does in his literature, according to Holmer, is to sketch the mode of life in which concepts acquire their particular meaning by showing the concerns and preoccupations they inform and in which they have their life. In this sense, what Kierkegaard does is to put language back into existence, and in so doing, he shows that "understanding" in such cases (such as understanding oneself) is a capacity in the sense that it is a personal achievement, a qualification of one's subjectivity. As Holmer writes in his "About Understanding," 173:

> Instead Kierkegaard is at pains to show us how these concepts work, how complex they are, and how far we are from understanding them rightly if we only describe them with that sort of learning which is 'indifferent.' By contrast he chooses another form and another set criteria that provide the appropriate context in which 'understanding' can take place. He is not writing out the understanding or providing a written defaition which can serve as the understanding; instead he is giving the words their employment, even their role in a linguistic context (as well as non-linguistic context). Then gaining the understanding is something to be done by the reader.

As we will note, this is one of the areas where Holmer sees a strong resemblance in Kierkegaard's and Wittgenstein's thinking.

self."[49] This seemingly obscure statement, which has been the subject of extended exposition and commentary in Kierkegaard scholarship, is treated
by Holmer as a straight-forward and succinct statement of the nature of
the self. What Kierkegaard is arguing here, according to Holmer, is that
the self is, in essence, a relating activity such that "there is only the activity
or the lack thereof, the relation or the lack thereof," and for this reason,
"there is nothing to see but only something to be."[50] In this sense, the self is
that which is constituted precisely as one is passionately concerned about
oneself. Holmer likens knowledge of the self to knowledge of God: for just
as God is never available as object but is always pure subject, so, too, the
self is known only in the activity of relating to oneself in this concerned
way. As he goes on to write: "To say the self is a 'relation' implies that it is
not a substance, not a material thing, neither the body nor the mind. To be
a self is to be a relating agency, putting together mind and body, future and
present, impulses and duties. Our thinking demands an identity between
thinking and its object, and there is no identity until the self as a perduring
relation comes into view."[51] To repeat Kierkegaard's perspective, then, the
self is precisely that which, in the process of consciously relating to itself,
constitutes itself over time as an enduring entity.

In language reminiscent of Kierkegaard's assessment of the Christian
faith in *Concluding Unscientific Postscript*, Holmer suggests that the self,
too, is not primarily a "what" but a "how" consisting of the wide variety
of activities by means of which one becomes conscious of oneself. All that
goes into making a human life what it is—emotions, pathos, wishes, wants,
hopes, concerns—these are the instruments that must be directed to the
task of self understanding.

> We get a self and something to understand only by constituting
> ourselves. We have to wish, to hope, to want, to love, to promise
> and more. By doing all of this we acquire a self. For the self is
> not a thing but a relation, that relates itself to itself. By wanting
> steadily and long, a kind of definition of the person ensues. We
> are knowable by the fact that we have always wanted this or that.
> We become clear even to ourselves, as to who and what we are, by
> the intensity and constancy of our wants, wishes and loves. And if

49. Kierkegaard, *Fear and Trembling*, 146.
50. Holmer, "About Being a Person," 63.
51. Holmer, "Post-Kierkegaardian Remarks," 14–15.

we have never wanted or desired with steadiness and intensity, it is also the case that our lives have scarcely any definition at all.[52]

The self as "the synthesizing agent" or "relating agency" bringing together emotions, will and reflection, mind and body, future and present, impulses and duties therefore includes all those things that go into creating an enduring identity over time: the willing of a goal for oneself, an emotionally rich concern over what one can be, a thoughtful assessment of what one already is. The self as a relation is, therefore, an ongoing activity, never completed once and for all. And because it concerns the quality of one's own existence, it is necessarily "passionate thinking, not disinterested, not theoretical."[53]

It is precisely because the self is a "how" rather than a "what" that, according to Holmer "the burden of Kierkegaard's literature is to activate the reader's concern about what he himself is . . ."[54] What Kierkegaard's literature shows for Holmer is that achieving self-hood is neither a biological necessity nor simply a sociological attainment, but rather must be a "task" which one consciously assumes for oneself: "Kierkegaard causes us to see in the manifold of his literature that being a human individual requires us also to become agents of our own selfhood. We have to learn to think our existence. We have to become conscious of ourselves and develop a passionate concern about the quality of our lives."[55]

From the perspective of this view of the self, the various stages or spheres of existence illustrate the primary options within which the self seeks to attain and secure an enduring identity. It must be noted, however, that this "Christian psychological exposition," of the self, under the pseudonym, "Anti-Climacus," is part of Kierkegaard's larger literary project, and as such is forwarded in keeping with his understanding of "indirect communication."[56] Although the balance of our presentation concerns the first issue, a few comments in specific reference to this last topic may be helpful at this point.

52. Holmer, "About Being a Person," 69.

53. Holmer, "Post-Kierkegaardian Remarks," 15.

54. Ibid.

55. Ibid., 14.

56. The full title of *The Sickness Unto Death* includes the subtitle "A Christian Psychological Exposition for Edification and Awakening." In addition to the author's name, "Anti-Climacus," Kierkegaard's name is included as editor.

6. Indirect Communication

Even when Kierkegaard is most abstract and conceptual, Holmer does not view him as a metaphysician or purveyor of a "system"; rather, as Holmer straightforwardly notes, "Kierkegaard chose to do philosophy by examples."[57] As he goes on to note: "Instead of making the ordinary give-and-take of everyday life a manifestation or a 'symbol' or a representation' of something profound and deep, Kierkegaard believed that these examples are all there is . . . A philosopher who wants to think about matters of ethics and religion must begin with these, not with abstract concepts. The examples are the thing, and this is why Kierkegaard begins with them."[58]

Despite the somewhat obtuse nature of his reflections in such works as *The Sickness Unto Death*, Kierkegaard's use of examples and practice of "indirect communication" are central to pseudonymous authorship and linked with Kierkegaard's overall purpose in his literature. According to Holmer, Kierkegaard understood that a direct attack on the prevailing Hegelian philosophy of his time would simply be viewed as another philosophical doctrine and therefore, by its very form, would communicate a misunderstanding. It is for this reason, according to Holmer, that Kierkegaard employed an "indirect" mode of communication by means of his pseudonymous authorship.

As Holmer notes, while each author and work is distinct, there is an overarching purpose at work: "Kierkegaard's pseudonymous works do play a role in the literature as a whole, and that purpose has a 'telos,' not identical with what is stated in any single book. The whole literature 'shows,' after a while, by its very shape and the uses that are appropriate, what cannot be said without falsifying that purpose. That purpose is a realization in the life of a reader and not one more theory about human lives."[59]

In Holmer's view, Kierkegaard is not attempting to disguise or conceal himself through the use of pseudonyms; rather, the use of this device is connected to the fact that "he thought it preposterous to invoke his own authority for something like a fundamental mode of living and erected ideal 'personae' really to divert attention from himself and to maximize the activation of the capabilities and power of each of his readers. The intrusion of the author's authority would vitiate the creation and sustaining of

---

57. Holmer, "Kierkegaard and Philosophy," 6.

58. Ibid., 7.

59. Holmer, "Post-Kierkegaardian Remarks," 11.

an authorizing activity on the part of the reader."[60] From this perspective, psuedonymns were not used primarily to secure anonymity but rather "to allow for a development in literary form of the ideal proportions of various views of life."[61] As idealized characterizations presented in the aesthetic, ethical, ethico-religious, and Christian modes, the "stages on life's way" are not strictly chronological nor are they life-phases, but rather, as Holmer understands it, "they are more like ways that lives get formed, when choice is exercised, when decisions are made, when ideas are taken seriously, when pathos is educated."[62] The pseudonymous literature works by presenting characterizations which are more distinct than historical personages; they are, instead, ideal, even exaggerated types. This literary device enables Kierkegaard to present the fundamental issues, conflicts, and polemical postures of each of the stages and bring them into a sharper focus in a way that "both compresses human circumstances and distills the consequences of the forms of life we all choose, so that we get a more acute picture of what is involved. . . . the literature clarifies both by its idealizations and by shortening the period between antecedent choices and their kinds of consequences.[63]

As an indirect form of communication, Kierkegaard's pseudonymous works stand in contrast to those philosophical views which assume the problems of daily life to be simply problems of cognitive knowledge. By directing attention away from a systematic resolution of these problems and refusing to answer these questions directly merely to increase the store of human knowledge "about" these issues, Kierkegaard's indirection served as "a discipline upon intellectual promiscuity, which forced men again to the awareness of what it means to live."[64] In this sense, Kierkegaard's use of indirect communication "shows" rather than simply states the alternative views of life "without inventing a foundation, a ground, a common court of appeal, an objective standard, and so on. He leaves it to the reader to decide."[65] What philosophy has proposed to communicate directly (as, for example, in Hegel's philosophy), Kierkegaard believes must be indirectly

60. Ibid.

61. Holmer, "Kierkegaard and Ethical Theory," 159.

62. Holmer, "Post-Kierkegaardian Remarks," 13.

63. Ibid.

64. Holmer, "Kierkegaard and Philosophy," 17.

65. Ibid., 18. As we will later discuss in more detail this notion of "showing"—as opposed to "saying"—in regard to ethical and religious forms of life, suggests a similarity between Kierkegaard's work and Wittgenstein's early and later philosophy.

rendered because "the responsibility for a view of life can never be anyone's but each man's himself."[66]

Lastly, Holmer agrees with Kierkegaard's view that indirect communication is linked to the very content of the Christian message: "This matter of indirect communication is given a multiform interpretation in Kierkegaard's literature. In the last analysis he so understands it to be appropriate to the very heart of Christianity, for here is God helpless in the hands of enemies, even on a cross . . ."[67] Because it involves the transformation of one's subjectivity and not merely the conveying of information, the content of the Christian message is such that there can be no direct transference or communication. In place of such direct communication of facts what is required in both ethical and Christian communication is a process of "double reflection" wherein what is communicated must become embodied in the life of the hearer. Where factual information may be part of this communication, in order for the authentic communication to be achieved, the hearer or learner must reflect upon this information in such a way that it produces the capacity for a new self understanding. In reference to the content of the Christian message, it is not enough that one merely reiterate doctrines concerning Jesus Christ; rather for authentic understanding to be achieved, these doctrines become the occasion for the development of new capacities of self-understanding, discipline and action. In this way, as Holmer sees it, Kierkegaard's use of indirect communication is not merely as an optional literary form but instead is directly connected to both the content and the purpose of his literature. It is because Kierkegaard seeks to communicate not information but a capability, not knowledge about, but a capacity for ethical and religious life that he employs the intentional literary technique and philosophical method termed "indirect communication."

7. Spheres of Existence and Forms of Life

According to Holmer, what Kierkegaard seeks to demonstrate by his "stages or spheres of existence is that the various forms of life differ in the degree to which they require and sustain self-reflection, self-concern, and self-intending."[68] In this sense, for Holmer, they represent kinds of subjectivity

---

66. Ibid., 19.
67. Ibid.
68. Holmer, "Post-Kierkegaardian Remarks," 14.

or what, in keeping with Wittgenstein, may be termed "forms of life."[69] In the case of the aesthetic stage, for example, Kierkegaard demonstrates that this form of life "may be constituted by accident, by 'raw material,' by chance, and by the fortuitous concatenation of circumstances that a family or an environment provides."[70] In Kierkegaard's view, this stage, dominated by the twin poles of pain and pleasure, breeds its own dissatisfaction and eventually leads to despair precisely because it is unable to develop and sustain an enduring self. Indeed, it may even be said that this stage represents a kind of "pre-self" modality insofar as it avoids the actual task of becoming a self.[71]

In contrast, as Holmer interprets Kierkegaard's position, the ethical mode of life is one which makes of selfhood a genuine pursuit, which then becomes the task around which the individual's passion is focused and organized. The essence of the ethical sphere is to take up the task of selfhood by seeking to constitute and justify one's life in accord with what are viewed to be universal laws and precepts. In this sphere the concepts of "rightness" and "duty" are paramount and it is by means of these ethical concepts that a "proneness to intend oneself is thereby given form and morphology."[72] Holmer goes on to note that as this takes shape a kind of "logic" of ethical

69. Holmer, of course, is not alone in seeing similarities between Kierkegaard's stages and Wittgenstein's notion of "forms of life." Noting Wittgenstein's view that "to imagine a language is to imagine a form of life," Stanley Cavell in his *Must We Mean What We Say?*, 67, contends that "to understand an utterance religiously you have to be able to share its perspective. . . . The religious is a Kierkegaardian Stage of life; and I suggest it should be thought of as a Wittgensteinian form of life." We should also note, however, that significant interpreters of Wittgenstein would challenge the view that Kierkegaard's "stages" may properly be conceived as analogous to what Wittgenstein means by "forms of life." For these interpreters, Kierkegaard's stages are too generalized and exaggerated to serve as concrete "forms of life." For our purposes, however, what is of chief significance is Holmer's view that Kierkegaard's way of doing philosophy, like Wittgenstein's, employs examples and analyzes important concepts by placing them within the context of a life setting. Kierkegaard's stages need not be viewed precisely as "forms of life" in Wittgenstein's sense of the phrase for these similarities to be noted.

70. Holmer, "Post-Kierkegaardian Remarks," 14.

71. Holmer seems to suggest this perspective in his treatment of the stages in his "Post-Kierkegaardian Remarks," inasmuch as he does not deal with Kierkegaard's statement about the self as "a relation which relates itself to itself" until examining the ethical stage. This interpretation is, in turn, corroborated by the fact that the pseudonym "Anti-Climacus," Kierkegaard's "Christian author," is the author of *The Sickness Unto Death*, where this treatment of the self is presented. Holmer also notes that a similar view of the self is presented by "Judge Wilhelm" in *Either/Or*.

72. Holmer, "About Being a Person," 65.

behavior and thought is disclosed. The descriptive rendering of this "logic" or what might be termed the "grammar" of a particular form of life is, in Holmer's view, a significant point of commonality shared by Søren Kierkegaard and Ludwig Wittgenstein. In turn, as we have suggested and will further explore in subsequent chapters, this uniting of ethical and logical concerns is a consistent theme in Holmer's own thought.

It is in reference to the significance of the distinctive concepts in a particular sphere that one of Holmer's constructive uses of Kierkegaard's thought is seen. As Holmer notes: "But with the ethical comes also a host of other concepts and these in turn become a good part of ethical behavior itself, and not just its cause or its symptom. The thought pattern itself is both a pattern for the deeds as well as part of ethical behavior."[73] Here the similarity between Kierkegaard's thought and the philosophy of the later Wittgenstein is suggested by Holmer, inasmuch as both these thinkers recognize the fundamental "linguisticality" of human existence and pay close attention to the connection between language use, concepts and the "form of life" of which they are part. It is this perceived logical connection between the meaning of a concept and the form of life in which it is embedded that underlies both Kierkegaard's understanding of the task of philosophy and his own way of doing philosophical reflection. Because ethics and religion have application first and foremost to individuals within the context of everyday existence, according to Holmer, a fundamental tenet of Kierkegaard's understanding of philosophy is that what philosophers must do to handle the problems of ethics and religion is to look very closely at existing people. As Holmer puts it: "Instead of making the ordinary give and take of life a 'manifestation' or 'symbol' or a 'representation' of something profound or deep, Kierkegaard believes that these examples are all there are."[74] For this reason, according to Holmer, Kierkegaard's examples "are not simply illustrations of more abstract points," but both philosophy and "a reminder of where the examples worth philosophizing about are."[75] This same emphasis on attending to ordinary examples and seeing the way concepts are connected to a form of life are primary themes in Holmer's appreciation of Wittgenstein's thought. But, as we will see, where Holmer learns from Wittgenstein the importance of describing the grammar and

---

73. Ibid., 65.
74. Holmer, "Kierkegaard and Philosophy," 7
75. Ibid., 8

logic of particular language uses, he sees in Kierkegaard a concern with what he terms the "logic of subjectivity" and a larger "grammar of life."

As Holmer presents it, what Kierkegaard's examples of forms of life in the aesthetic, ethical and religious spheres do is to show a variety of ways of life by highlighting both the similarities and significant differences between them. There is no attempt to resolve these differences in a higher synthesis, but rather the intent to show that the real wisdom of life—discerned by attending to the details of how persons exist, how they make decisions and how they act—"has to be purchased with effort, deep passion, deep caring; and it cannot be summarized and disseminated at second-hand."[76]

What Holmer's interpretation of Kierkegaard's work taken as a whole argues is that a fundamental critique of philosophy is forwarded not only by means of the content of this literature, but also by its form. For what Kierkegaard's literature shows is that if one is properly going to philosophize about issues of ethics and religion, "the examples have to be multiple, the concepts numerous, the literature a little more casual, insinuating into the hard cases, and not formal and abstract."[77]

In light of Kierkegaard's critique of the philosophy of his own time, Holmer goes on to criticize contemporary philosophy as well:

> Most writers on the philosophy of religion and even ethics have rather slight sympathy for the nuances of spiritual attitudes and their related concepts. Their description of moral and spiritual attitudes is very much like those naive paintings which depict a landscape in general, to fit everything but finally nothing. Therefore, to describe religious faith as devotion to an ideal, without distinguishing the differences between obligations, never bothering with the all-important matter of the 'how' involved, is about as illuminating and intellectually satisfying as it would be to describe man as an animal and leave out any further specification.[78]

According to Holmer, Kierkegaard's examples offer a more precise intellectual orientation on the actual variety of ethical and religious behavior than any abstract, generalized treatment makes possible. What Kierkegaard's procedure achieves thereby is a subtle and nuanced view of how people actually think and act in the arena of ethical and religious concern. It is

76. Ibid., 9.
77. Ibid.
78. Ibid.

in this sense that the work of Kierkegaard's literature is to show the "logic" and "grammar" of a given sphere of existence, and even, a "grammar of life."

8. The Breach of Consciousness

To return to Kierkegaard's notion of the ethical sphere of life, part of its distinctive logic is that the rules and laws that become part of the conceptual framework are not private or arbitrary, but must be public, universal and statable. It is for this reason, for example, that the story of Abraham and his journey to Mt. Moriah, recounted in *Fear and Trembling*, is so problematic. For the willingness to sacrifice his son, Isaac, to God is no mere lapse of ethical consciousness, but a "breach" of this consciousness and its conceptuality of universal and statable rules. What is confronted here is, in fact, a paradox which no amount of discursive knowledge can resolve, a chasm "which no enlarging the cognitive conceptual scheme" can bridge.[79] The issue at stake is simply outside the categories available within the sphere of ethicality and thus a crisis of consciousness, a crisis of self-understanding ensues. In *Fear and Trembling*, through the voice of pseudonym "Johannes de Silento," Kierkegaard charts the contours of the movement, and the crisis effecting the movement, from an ethical to a religious consciousness.

In keeping with our earlier observations about the "linguisticality" of a form of life, Holmer describes the movement from an ethical to religious consciousness by noting that "becoming religious is, in part, a matter of learning a new language."[80] The rules of reasoning, in the case of the ethical sphere, by formalizing one's wants and duties, also provide and form one's reasons for living in a particular way. These rules of reasoning are part of the "grammar" of how one lives and the criteria for these rules do not have an existence apart from the way in which they become manifest in the way one lives: "'Sense' and 'meaning,' 'order' and 'rational' are all parasitic upon a grammar that our lives lay down."[81] In other words, as we have noted, such terms have their specific meaning in light of the uses they are put to within a particular form of life. It is this kind of "logic of terms" that, in Holmer's view, is the proper discernment of philosophers, and as we will see, this same perspective underlies Kierkegaard's connection of truth and subjectivity in the sphere of religious faith. As he writes: "Such an understanding

79. Holmer, "About Being a Person," 66.
80. Holmer, *Theology and the Scientific Study of Religion*, 161.
81. Holmer, "About Being a Person," 71.

does allow a linguistic expression, but the linguistic expression, in turn, is not the understanding but it is 'of' it. Thus, 'truth is subjectivity' is a piece of philosophy. It is not a super theory. It is more like what Wittgenstein would have called a 'grammatical remark.' Therefore, its use is, again, to call attention to the way to think about moral religious matters—not the least of which is how to use the word 'truth' in these special areas of concern."[82]

At a later point we will further examine the importance that Holmer attaches to ethicality and a morality of the virtues as preparatory, and even the necessary preparation, for understanding the condition that Christianity addresses. This is part of Holmer's "morphology of the life of Christian belief" and clearly informed by Kierkegaard's "stages" as well. But here we note Kierkegaard's point that there is no simple transition or mediation between the stage of ethicality to that of specifically religious faith. Although for Kierkegaard the ethical stage is that point at which the task of becoming a self is engaged, it remains qualitatively different from religious faith.

As Holmer presents it, the move from the sphere of ethicality to that of specifically religious faith requires a new sort of consciousness of the self, a new logic and grammar. Rather than the concepts of right and wrong, duty and universality, new concepts of determinative significance emerge. Or rather one might say these same concepts undergo a shift in meaning as they move from one sphere of existence to another. For in the religious realm, "duty" transcends its purely ethical meaning because it concerns one's duty to God. The crisis that ensues in the conflict between these two conceptions of duty is the crucible within which self-understanding is transformed. This is a crisis which cannot be resolved by appeal to outside criteria because the sphere of existence or way of life is itself the source of such criteria.

For this reason, according to Holmer, one problem that Kierkegaard addresses by means of the story of Abraham and Isaac in *Fear and Trembling* and throughout his pseudonymous literature is also the problem of various philosophical "-isms." Such all-encompassing views propose "bringing everything under a single conceptual scheme" as a means of avoiding the paradox implicit in the Abraham story, and it is this attempt to "place all dichotomies within an underlying synthesis and all disunities within a deep and invisible unity," which is the issue at stake in Kierkegaard's critique of Hegel's philosophy.[83] According to Holmer, Hegel's move to resolve all

82. Holmer, "Post-Kierkegaardian Remarks," 12.
83. Holmer, "About Being a Person," 67.

apparent paradoxes as a phase in the unfolding of an all-inclusive cosmic consciousness represents for Kierkegaard "a confusion introduced by thinking, not just by the absence of thinking."[84] To repeat what we have noted earlier, the error of such allegedly scholarly-scientific views is that they "transfer our passion from the effort to become true persons to the effort of searching out the right theory or objective truth about persons."[85] Although an authentic ethical perspective shares the personal and passionate concern with becoming a self that is the mark of religious faith, those efforts to reduce religious faith to ethics or to ground Christianity in a rational ethical imperative are mistaken.

According to Holmer, Kierkegaard's fundamental point is that there is no single system or conceptual scheme which can resolve this breach in consciousness just as there is no growth in self-understanding by the subsuming of the self into an all encompassing "objective" system. Where Kierkegaard does allow for a system of logic, he denies the possibility of a "system of existence" in the sense that any "objective" approach can resolve the basic issue of what it is to be an existing human being or the more specific issue of an ethical versus a religious form of life. It is for this reason that Kierkegaard is at pains to show the distortion that occurs when a concept such as "truth" is divorced from the specific context in which the issue is raised and why "subjectivity" is the truth when one is faced with the objectivity uncertainty of faith.

9. Truth and Subjectivity

As Holmer understands it, Kierkegaard denies that there is a superior philosophic concept of truth, a meta-concept and part of the point of his reflection on truth and subjectivity is to show that the seriousness and gravity of a passionate (or moral) subject makes such a meta-concept, "this philosophic concept, gratuitous . . . superfluous at best and distracting at the worst"[86] That is to say, the concept of truth in regard to ethical and religious matters simply cannot be understood apart from the context in which it is at stake for an existing human being. In place of this "objective approach," Kierkegaard speaks to the issue of understanding oneself by attacking "our feelings, our indifference, by stimulating self-concern and

84. Holmer, "Post-Kierkegaardian Remarks," 16.

85. Ibid., 16.

86. Holmer, "Kierkegaard and Philosophy," 12.

magnifying our anxiety, our despair and our guilt. For these, rather than being only problems to be resolved, also have to become the very means and motives for seeking a new life. What science and scholarship ask us to bracket for the sake of understanding, Kierkegaard asks us to augment for the sake of bringing the self to birth."[87]

For Kierkegaard, it is precisely this conflict, and the objective uncertainty of faith as a way of life, that must be emphasized. According to Holmer, Kierkegaard's writings work "by making the case for objective uncertainty glaringly, by stirring self consciousness, by clarifying despair so that it at least is acknowledged, by proposing anew the idealities, like happiness, forgiveness, peace of mind, hope, so that they will indeed attract one to a high calling."[88] This is the work of *Concluding Unscientific Postscript* and the pseudonymous literature as a whole. As Holmer notes:

> This then is how Christianity becomes commensurate with persons. For only when one is desperate, even broken-hearted about oneself, does faith begin to cohere. Only when we are sick and need the physician will the life of faith acquire any plausibility. . . . But once the subjectivity is developed, a rich subjectivity cultivated, then and only then will any kind of relation between the finite and infinite, between God and man, even become likely. In Christian terms, man's need for God is his highest perfection. That need for God will not occur unless there are crises in the subjective life.[89]

It is here, once again, that the centrality of what it means to be a self, at stake in the whole of Kierkegaard's literature, is elucidated. For the issue of "truth" in relation to Christianity is not the truth of doctrine, but that of becoming a "true self." As we noted earlier, in Holmer's words, "to be a self is to have made the self:"

> We get a self and something to understand only by constituting ourselves. We have to wish, to hope, to want, to love, to promise and more. By doing all of this we acquire a self. For the self is not a thing but a relation that relates itself to itself. By wanting steadily and long, a kind of definition of the person ensues. We are knowable by the fact that we have always wanted this or that. We become clear even to ourselves, as to who and what we are, by the intensity and constancy of our wants, wishes and loves. And if

87. Holmer, "Post-Kierkegaardian Remarks," 19.

88. Ibid., 21.

89. Ibid.

we have never wanted or desired with steadiness and intensity, it is also the case that our lives have scarcely any definition at all. We never arrive at the goal of being a true self. This is Kierkegaard's point through his entire authorship. . . .[90]

According to Holmer, there is no universal or objective vantage point, no one logical point of view, outside of morality or outside of religion, that can provide certainty for our decision. The implication of this, for Holmer as well as for Kierkegaard, is that "there is no truth waiting to be discovered that tells us what we ought to do . . . instead to be a self is to have a capacity for self-clarification only via the bloody and long way."[91]

What Kierkegaard's *Fear and Trembling* and other pseudonymous works do is to show us "via the category of the stages that there is a kind of morphology to our lives" which is neither random nor simply fortuitous. And yet as Holmer makes clear, to make the move from the ethical realm to the religious is a kind of understanding that cannot be delivered to us by a book or system of thought. In this realm the issues at stake can only be resolved by the individual in "fear and trembling." As Holmer goes on to note, Kierkegaard's philosophy, "insofar as he can be said to have one at all, is not the truth one needs; rather it is like an account of the relations between pathos and thought, emotion and belief, that make up the way in which we do form our lives."[92] What is required, as Holmer puts it, is a "deep kind of activity" where one's consciousness of oneself "is moved by the wanting, wishing and caring that made Abraham faithful and the father of faith."[93] What Kierkegaard tries to show, both in his stages, and the breaches of consciousness which separate them, is that there is no resolution for the fundamental issues of self-understanding and identity that can be provided to one outside of one's own passionate search for the truth.

10. Christianity and Truth

In all of his reflections on Kierkegaard's thought, Holmer makes clear that, in his view, Kierkegaard is "first and last, a religious and Christian writer."[94] Although this does not prevent Kierkegaard from noting the "logic and

90. Holmer, "About Being a Person," 69.

91. Ibid., 73.

92. Holmer, Post-Kierkegaardian Remarks," 10.

93. Holmer, "About Being a Person," 76.

94. Holmer, "Post-Kierkegaardian Remarks," 20.

rhythm" of the subjective life and examining the intricacies of human psychology, Kierkegaard brings another concern to bear on these issues. As Holmer writes: "This is, plainly, that Christianity provides, through the Bible a kind of self-knowledge that one gets nowhere else. It is as though the Bible also educates us, not by providing the truths and the right doctrine, but by being a mirror in which we see ourselves. Then the religious life becomes an adventure in self-knowledge and not just a matter of believing. God in Christ even supplies a new capacity in people."[95]

It is in *Concluding Unscientific Postscript* that Kierkegaard addresses the issue of subjectivity in regard to ethico-religious truth most directly. Here, through the pseudonym, "Johannes Climacus," Kierkegaard poses the question of "the objective truth of Christianity" and organizes this work around the issue of "how the subjectivity of the individual must be qualified in order that certain issues come to exist for him."[96] As Holmer summarizes it, "One matter that emerges is that the familiar way of saying that a given teaching—say, either in moral discourse or in Christian teaching, is true, itself gets to be suspicious."[97] So it is, according to Holmer, that "Kierkegaard develops, in some independence of the logical and epistemological traditions of the nineteenth century, deep misgivings about taking sentences out of moral and religious usage and bracketing them."[98]

As Holmer understands it, throughout Kierkegaard's literature—"almost like a long book with many chapters"—there is an argument going on against pan-logistic thought. In the course of this argument, Kierkegaard shows, for example, that the use of "faith" in religious contexts is not really like "belief" or "faith" when used in other contexts; and as Holmer adds, "then there is 'truth' used in a religious context. Jesus saying 'I am the truth. . .'" quite clearly does not use the same concept 'truth' as in 'I speak the truth; I assure you I am not lying.'"[99] What Kierkegaard does is to look at the concept of truth within the contexts of ethical and religious spheres of existence inasmuch as these differing spheres can be understood as realms of discourse or forms of life.

It is in light of our discussion of Kierkegaard's understanding of the self that the meaning of Kierkegaard's phrase, "truth is subjectivity" may

95. Ibid., 20.
96. Ibid., 19.
97. Holmer, "Kierkegaard and Philosophy," 11.
98. Ibid.
99. Ibid., 14.

finally be understood. As Holmer presents it, in the same sense that a self may be understood as a process rather than a thing, religious belief is a matter of the "how" rather than the "what." The focus in regard to matters of religion and ethics is not on the specific content of a doctrine or teaching so much as it is in the passionate commitment—infinite in the case of the objective uncertainty of faith in God—which is the relevant "truth" issue in these realms. In this sense, religious truth lies in the individual's subjectivity: "The point of religious language is not to communicate results as much as to stimulate the process of experience and thought which will reconstitute the human personality. Ethico-religious truth is, in other words, not a quality of the language itself but is rather the process, the striving of the human subject to be a definitive individual."[100]

As Holmer understands it, Kierkegaard defines religious truth not as sentences to be learned but as a "dynamic becoming of the self." Kierkegaard's position that the content of Christianity is passional rather than solely conceptual suggests to Holmer that "Kierkegaard felt a responsibility as an author to lead his reader out of his subjectivity and into the contemplation of objectivities only for the sake of the new subjectivity which Christian faith, hope and love are.[101]

This is not to disparage the importance of "objectivity" or an objective sense of the concept of truth in scientific and other scholarly discourse. But it is to say that this is not the only meaning of the concept of truth in reference to the Christian faith. As Holmer writes:

> When Christians speak of Jesus as the truth, of the Christian life as the true life, of the Bible as God's truth, they surely do not intend to say that becoming a Christian is a matter of learning true sentences. . . . Truth in the religious sense is not a quality of sentences at all. Religion and Christianity very clearly seek to make men true subjects. Religious truth is not connotative—it is denotative, indicating always that quality which men can aspire to. For objective truths about that quality are not that quality. There can be no substitute for being the truth, no matter what the quantity of truths we may possess.[102]

"Subjectivity," then, is the personal, passionate involvement and decision required in that area of human life which constitutes ethical and religious

---

100. Holmer, *Theology and the Scientific Study of Religion*, 199.

101. Ibid., 202.

102. Holmer, "Christianity and the Truth," 40.

concern. This concern with subjectivity, with "truth as subjectivity" is shared by moral concern and religious faith. In these spheres which have "an essential reference to the existence of the knower," the mode of apprehension is precisely the truth at issue.

However, "subjectivity" takes on a more specific meaning for Kierkegaard in relation to the "objective uncertainty" of the central content of the Christian faith—the doctrine of the "God-man." For faith is not merely the presence of an infinite passion directed toward becoming a self, but involves both passion and belief. In Kierkegaard's terms, truth here is the truth of an infinite passion directed toward an "eternal happiness." But specifically Christian faith is distinguished from other forms of passionate inwardness in regard to its "object." As "Johannes Climacus" writes in the *Postscript*, the inwardness of Christian faith is "specifically different from all other inwardness," in that "the how can correspond to only one thing, the absolute paradox."[103]

As distinguished from the infinite concern that it shares with the ethical sphere, faith is directed beyond concern with the self. As we read in the *Postscript*, "the analogy between faith and the ethical is found in the infinite interest . . . but the believer differs from the ethicist in being infinitely interested in the reality of another.[104] Thus, faith is distinguished from the ethical in light of its infinite interest in an "other"; in the case of Christianity this "other" is the absolute paradox of the God-man. That is to say, it is not the teachings but the person of Christ that is of primary concern:

> The object of faith is the reality of another and the relationship is one of infinite interest. The object of faith is not a doctrine, for then the relationship would be intellectual. . . . The object of faith is not a teacher with a doctrine, for when a teacher has a doctrine the doctrine is *eo ipso* more important that the teacher. The object of faith is the reality of the teacher, that the teacher really exists . . . The object of faith is thus God's reality in existence as a particular individual, the fact that God has existed as an individual human being.[105]

It is in this sense that we may say that for Kierkegaard there is a place for the "objective" content of the Christian faith. But it is precisely the character of this "what" that requires the "how" of faith wherein "truth is

103. Kierkegaard, *Concluding Unscientific Postscript*, 549.

104. Ibid., 288.

105. Ibid., 290–91.

subjectivity." The characterization of truth as subjectivity is therefore not a doctrine or theory on Kierkegaard's part, but as Holmer reads it, more in the order of a "grammatical remark" concerning the way the concept of truth operates, the proper use of the concept, in the realm of religious faith. For as Kierkegaard affirms in *Training in Christianity*, the truth of Christianity, the truth of the passionate concerned relationship with the God revealed in Christ, is the truth of "a way, a life," in which an individual becomes a true self: "Christ is the truth in such a sense that to be the truth is the only true explanation of what the truth is. . . . That is to say, the truth in the sense which Christ was the truth is not a sum of sentences, not a definition of concepts . . . but a life . . . Truth in its very being is the reduplication in me . . . is a life."[106]

Conclusion

As we have attempted to demonstrate, for Paul Holmer Kierkegaard's philosophy—particularly as evidenced in the pseudonymous literature—illustrates a distinctive way of conceiving and undertaking philosophical reflection. It is this way of viewing philosophy as "primarily a matter of clearing away the obstacles in the way of describing and understanding some very difficult matters," which, in Holmer's mind, links Kierkegaard's work with that of Ludwig Wittgenstein. As Holmer notes: "Philosophy has to be done in bits and pieces, in fragments (though rather large ones sometimes.) Philosophy is unscientific, according to *Concluding Unscientific Postscript*; but not 'unscientific' only in the ordinary sense of 'science.' Rather the aim is to show that here this reflection must be *uvidenskapelig*, non-systematic, insinuating and open to the study of pathos and passion as these also contribute to our own language, our aspirations, our morals and our religion."[107]

As we have seen, according to Holmer, Kierkegaard's literature portrays the "grammar" of the sphere of ethical concern and religious faith, showing the ruled usage of its convictional language; showing, that is, what kind of truth is asserted and made possible and what sort of qualification of the individual's self-understanding is required both for one to become a self and before a transition from one sphere of existence to another can take place. Through the content and the form of his literature what Kierkegaard

---

106. Kierkegaard, *Training in Christianity*, 204.
107. Holmer, "Kierkegaard and Philosophy," 13.

depicts "is the very grammar of the way we must live if we are to become true persons."[108]

As Holmer puts it, to be a self requires that wants and hopes, reflection and judgment, passions and attitudes are directed by a concern about the quality and meaning of one's life. Genuine ethical and religious knowledge cannot be delivered at second hand, for it is not knowledge "about" the self, but rather "of" the self. Living within the context of the contingencies and ambiguities of human existence, such knowledge does not happen through disinterested objectivity or detachment but only by means of passionate personal interest and involvement. In this sense, the self develops only as it grows in consciousness of itself and an enduring self-identity is achieved only as one has a passionate concern for the quality of one's life, in who one is and how one lives.

The various stages or spheres of existence which Kierkegaard delineates are for Holmer idealized descriptions of the primary options available to human consciousness. Kierkegaard's stages are not a "system of existence" but a detailed descriptive rendering of the ways human beings live and think. As employed by Kierkegaard, these stages provide a kind of mapping, or as Holmer terms it, a "morphology" of self-understanding. But as Holmer repeatedly emphasizes, "Kierkegaard's literature does not just represent or reproduce. It is designed to be the occasion for bringing the person and the self to birth."[109] In Holmer's view, Kierkegaard's entire authorship is primarily concerned with showing just how difficult and demanding the inwardness of faith is. In an age where aesthetic categories dominate and where objective knowledge is seen as the goal of human knowledge, taking his lead from Kierkegaard, Holmer calls for pathos and interest, remorse and repentance, hope and courage; calls, that is, for faith. And faith here is understood both in reference to the concern and rigor of the ethical life and the distinctiveness of it object. For both Holmer and Kierkegaard stress that even as the self is formed in self-consciousness it must also be related to that reality beyond the self which is never available as object but only as pure subject. Faith then is an objective uncertainty that cannot be mediated. And yet a "grammar of the faith" can be described and delineated showing how its convictional language works, what kind of truth it asserts or makes possible, and what sort of qualifications of the individual's self-understanding are required to grasp its truth. Faith, as this

---

108. Holmer, "Post-Kierkegaardian Remarks," 12.

109. Ibid., 13.

grammar reveals, is a passion, even a "happy passion." All this, I believe, Holmer learns from Kierkegaard. He then brings to bear his own insights and concerns—not least those influenced by his reading of Wittgenstein—to further an understanding of Kierkegaard's literature and to go on to describe the "morphology of the life of Christian belief."

Again, in keeping with the intent which Kierkegaard states directly in his journals and *Point of View for My Work as an Author*, the goal of Kierkegaard's reflective activity is "to make men aware of Christianity."[110] For both Kierkegaard and Holmer what it is to make one aware of Christianity is to show that "Christianity is subjectivity, an inner transformation, an actualization of inwardness" where faith is itself "the evidence, the witness, and conviction the motivation."[111] Holmer's interpretation of Kierkegaard's writings is one which acknowledges and elucidates the avowed intention of the author and, in keeping with this intent, itself serves as a continuing communication not of results but of the truth of a way of thought and action. This interpretation of Kierkegaard serves as an inducement for the reader to go precisely his or her own way by portraying the task of what it is to be a self, by encouraging a concern for the Absolute and by reminding one that in this realm, "the only proof there is, is faith."[112]

---

110. Kierkegaard, *Journals of Kierkegaard*, 175.

111. Kierkegaard, *Diary of Søren Kierkegaard*, 165.

112. Ibid., 163.

2

Thinking with Wittgenstein

"The work of the philosopher consists in assembling reminders for particular purposes."[1]

1. Introduction

As we have suggested in the previous chapter, while recognizing significant differences in the focus of their work, Paul Holmer sees an important affinity between the writings of Søren Kierkegaard and the philosophy of Ludwig Wittgenstein. Holmer recognized that the terms "logic" and "grammar" have a resemblance in Kierkegaard's and Wittgenstein's writings and his later work on Kierkegaard's thought bears the mark of his reading of Wittgenstein.[2] And it may be said that the balance of Holmer's later writings, and in particular his major work, *The Grammar of Faith*, are a kind of extended application of Wittgenstein's way of doing philosophy to some of the fundamental issues of theology. In this chapter we will explore in greater detail some aspects of Holmer's interpretation of Wittgenstein's philosophy and some of the implications of this way of doing philosophy for Christian theology. But given our concern with Holmer's appropriation of Wittgenstein's philosophy and its application to questions about the

---

1. Wittgenstein, *Philosophical Investigations*, part I, section 126.

2. Bell, *Grammar of the Heart*, xvi. In his introduction to the essays, Bell notes that Holmer early on recognized the full implications of Wittgenstein's work.

nature of religious language and belief, it may be helpful first to examine an example of Holmer's treatment of some of the same issues prior to his reading of Wittgenstein.[3]

2. The Nature of Religious Propositions

In an article first appearing in 1955 when he was teaching at the University of Minnesota, entitled "The Nature of Religious Propositions," Holmer addresses the issue of the cognitive status of religious beliefs.[4] This analysis and resolution illustrates an early treatment of some of the issues that

3. As Richard Bell notes in his introduction to *The Grammar of the Heart*, the various forms of logical empiricism and linguistic analysis exemplified in the 1955 publication of *New Essays in Philosophical Theology*, provide the context in which Holmer's early work on Kierkegaard and the nature of religious language and belief were written. In some of his early articles, e.g., "Philosophical Criticism and Christology," 88–100; "Kierkegaard and Religious Propositions," 135–45; and "Kierkegaard and Theology," 23–31, Holmer combines a linguistic analysis perspective with the insights of Kierkegaard. A strongly anti-metaphysical view is connected to Kierkegaard's notion of religious belief as expressive of a "possibility" for existence. From this perspective Holmer challenges a narrow empiricist and verificationist view of religious belief and the nature of its truth by noting that where philosophical analysis can disabuse us of the need for a metaphysical grounding of religious truth, there is still a "religious" task of actualizing the possibility. For example, as he writes in "Philosophical Criticism and Theology," 97–99: "To the extent that possibles are of passionate interest and concern, they are what we call 'ethical possibilities.' Ethicality is a concern with possibility for the sake of one's interest in the future. Some possible picture the anticipated future for us. . . . It seems to me that Jesus Christ can be construed as God because he is a kind of ever relevant possibility. . . . The limited task of theology is to convert Jesus Christ into a 'possible'—a conceivable alternative mode of life and a mode about which one can discourse. The task for any man as a Christian is, religiously understood, much loftier; for it is to convert the possibility into the actuality of one's own life. This is the role of faith and hope and love."

4. Holmer, "The Nature of Religious Propositions," first published in *The Review of Religion*, 136–49; reprinted *Religious Language and the Problem of Religious Knowledge*, 233–47. We will use this later version of the article in our citations. In "Kierkegaard and Religious Propositions," 138–42, we see Holmer's use of Kierkegaard's thought in addressing the questions raised by the linguistic analysis of religious beliefs: "The attempt to make religion a cognitive enterprise by making God-sentences philosophically cognitive or metaphysically cognitive is vitiated by this analysis. The hope is and always has been that the truth-claim of such sentences is intrinsic to the sentence—i.e., an objective quality. . . . Actually, the truth-claim of such sentences presupposes certain dispositional properties in the thinker, so that one might say that the sentence does not produce the belief as much as it presupposes it. . . . for being a Christian is not having a cognitive relation to Jesus Christ and his passion but rather is a matter of having a noncognitive and passionate relation to Jesus Christ."

Holmer will return to in his *The Grammar of Faith*. What is of note here is Holmer's attempt to do justice to both the cognitive and "non-cognitive" aspects of religious belief. But as we will see, this treatment also suggests a kind of bifurcation of religious belief into these two separate components. Wittgenstein's notions of the distinctive grammar and logic of particular language games and his understanding of language use being connected to a "form of life" will later help Holmer more adequately to articulate some of the same themes he strikes in this early article. Wittgenstein's reflections move Holmer to see the way that what he earlier terms the cognitive and non-cognitive components of language are intimately interconnected and interwoven in a complex of activities and behavior. In this later view, it is not so easy to divide these two aspects because they are both part of the grammar of the language of faith.

In taking up the question, "Are religious beliefs cognitive?" Holmer examines some of the common responses to this issue. The first involves a kind of translation of religious beliefs into a philosophical conceptuality which is seen to provide the cognitive status otherwise missing from religious belief: "In this . . . kind of understanding, the achievement is among others the translation of religious sentences into an even more abstract linguistic system, and the extent to which they can thus be translated is the extent to which they are true."[5] The assumption here is that there is a single and necessary epistemological standpoint or cognitive ground to which all propositions are referable. This has been the perspective, for example, of what Holmer terms "supernaturalistic philosophies," which construe moral and religious sentences by analogy with sentences descriptive of nature. But with the demise of such philosophical systems a second response has become more typical.

According to this second view, religious sentences do not meet the basic criteria of cognition in terms of verifiability or falsifiability and are therefore simply meaningless. A variation, which still denies cognitive status to religious belief, is to say that such beliefs are merely emotive, expressing internal convictions or feelings. But according to Holmer, "it has been irresponsible thinking which has led many technical philosophers who have been otherwise known for their care and precision to insist, without careful analysis, that all religious sentences are simply nonsensical."[6]

---

5. Holmer, "The Nature of Religious Propositions," 234.
6. Ibid.

A third response, often proposed from the side of religion, is to view religious faith as trust or confidence rather than belief. Yet this, too, denies real cognitive status to religious beliefs and Holmer notes the similar conclusions reached both by this and the second position:

> In the latter instance, then, one denies cognition in religious sentences for the sake of faith understood as a quality of a man. In the former instance, one denies the cognition in religious sentences for the sake of intellectual consistency. But in both cases, the cognitive status of religious sentences in denied and the endeavor to describe the subject's religious act of belief by analogy with cognitive acts in intentionally decried. . . . This is the point toward which kinds of positivists and some radical fideistic Protestants seem to converge.[7]

In light of the problematic posed by both sides, what Holmer proposes is a careful analysis of religious beliefs. He does this by challenging the false analogy, on the one hand, drawn between religious belief and cognitive belief. To those who would equate religious faith with assent to propositions, he argues, "even the most avid adherents of creeds have known that assent to the truth claims of sentences is not a sufficient personal qualification to make one religious."[8] On the other hand, to those who attend to only the "personal qualities" involved in religious beliefs, he argues that "religious sentences are cognitive, but in some peculiar ways."[9]

Holmer recognizes the pertinence of the critique of religious beliefs in light of the tendency of traditional theology to claim cognitive status without distinguishing the sense in which the beliefs may be said to have this status; he also agrees that religiosity is "primarily a quality of persons, not of sentences," and that "perhaps religious belief is not analogous to cognitive belief," but goes on to observe that one can concede these points and still recognize a cognitive content in the religious sentences.[10] The important question for Holmer, then, is how the personal qualifications of the religious life are related to the act of assenting to the truth of sentences, and what beliefs are appropriately conceived in terms of such cognitive assent.

Holmer challenges the view held by both sides that the cognitive act of believing a religious sentence is equivalent to what we mean by religious

7. Ibid., 236–37.
8. Ibid., 235.
9. Ibid., 237.
10. Ibid.

faith. He notes that both theologians and philosophers have shared in this confusion, the one by equating assent with faith, the other by denying cognition in light of the alleged non-cognitive "personality" dimension in religious faith. Holmer suggests the similarity here with what is sometimes posed in terms of the "is" and the "ought" in religious belief, observing that "the confusion has been between the statement of truth (the 'is') and the consequences that knowing the truth is supposed to effect (the 'ought'). Without noting that the nature of the transition from an objective and disinterested apprehension of true sentences to a subjective quality, called being religious is not itself an implication nor a *natural* movement to be described as a relation of cause to effect, the distinction intrinsic to the peculiarity of religious sentences is thereby blurred.[11]"

"Religious sentences," according to Holmer, "are cognitive, but in a manner which begs elucidation." It is this elucidation that Holmer proposes in his answer that religious sentences "are cognitive of a possible way of construing one's life and daily existence."[12] Holmer distinguishes here between truths about actualities and truths about possibilities: the future is encountered and conceived only as a possibility since it does not yet exist; but a possibility may be described and therefore sentences concerning it may be judged true or false. Here the issue of truth is a cognitive one, namely, the truth (or falsity) of a sentence.

Holmer quickly notes, however, that to speak of cognitive truth in this sense is not peculiarly religious. The competency to conceive of future possibilities and entertain them is not uniquely religious. In addition, Holmer argues that even if the content of the sentence about a possibility is "religious" (e.g. a description of heaven or the converted life of a Christian), to agree to its truth is merely to agree that the sentence is a true description of the possibility; it is not the same as choosing it or equivalent to what religion speaks of in terms of faithfulness or righteousness. Therefore, Holmer concludes, "to the degree that religious sentences are about future possibilities, they can be cognitive and true, but that knowledge of this truth is not intrinsically religious."[13]

Holmer adds that there are factual claims that religions make. And in his view, such statements of alleged factual matters must be judged according to the same standards that any empirical statements are judged.

11. Ibid., 237–38.
12. Ibid., 238.
13. Ibid., 239.

He does, however, challenge the proclivity—represented by both religious apologists and their opposite—to lump together all such statements and claim that "all of any group of sentences about matters of fact must be true together or otherwise false together."[14]

But Holmer goes on to note that there is a kind of factual claim that is "intrinsic" to some religious statements. What he has in mind are those religions—Judaism, Christianity and Islam—that make cognitive claims about historical events and relate these to the cognitive claims about what Holmer has termed "possibilities." In these cases a historical figure or event is claimed to be the disclosure of a possible way of existing. To the extent that these are factual claims about historical events, they are both cognitive and subject to the criteria of all sentences about matters of fact. However, this again does not mean that assent to their truth is religious belief. It may be said that for such historical religions religious faith does suppose that one believe in the propositions expressing the basic historical claims, e.g., that Jesus did exist, but, as we have noted, this is not a religious belief. Nor, according to Holmer is such a belief, even combined with assent to the truth of the description of the possibility realized in the historical person or event, equivalent to religious belief. For Holmer, the distinguishing characteristic of the "religious act of faith or belief" is that "it requires not simply that I hold certain sentences to be true, but rather that I am becoming the possibility thus described."[15] This second aspect, according to Holmer, can be described as non-cognitive, but it may presuppose the cognitive beliefs described earlier. It is the "becoming of the possibility," as "an interest, an enthusiasm, a passion," that distinguishes religious faith from cognitive belief. In this sense, it is the passionate pursuit for the possibility which may be cognitively described which characterizes religious faith. As Holmer writes: "it seems clarifying, to me at least, to distinguish the cognitive sentences, admitting their religious neutrality whatever their religious use, and then also to separate the cognitive act of belief from the religious act of belief as objectivity is separated from subjectivity, as contemplation is from enthusiasm.[16]

As Holmer summarizes it, the confusions around the cognitive status of religious beliefs are the result of the two tendencies that may be described as "insisting upon the importance of the cognition of a (religious)

14. Ibid.
15. Ibid., 242
16. Ibid., 243.

possibility, religious faith becomes confused with cognitive belief; insisting on the non-cognitive aspect of faith, religious sentences are mistakenly assumed to be non-cognitive."[17] But as we have seen, for Holmer, the distinctively religious component is the passionate enthusiasm and interest in realizing the possibility, and therefore, when confronted with a possibility that may be cognitively described "to translate the sentences into this non-cognitive and passionate context is to put the sentence to a truly religious use."[18] And as Holmer emphasizes, even though the dimensions of cognition and faith can be distinguished in regard to a particular belief, the stress is on the later, "on reduplicating and becoming."[19] Beyond this, according to Holmer, there is no a priori way or ultimate metaphysical perspective or court of appeal by reference to which one can decide between the possibilities described.

This, then, is Holmer's response to the question of the cognitive status of religious belief. It illustrates an early treatment of some of the issues that he will return to in his *The Grammar of Faith* and elsewhere. But as we hope to show in our examination of Holmer's interpretation and use of Wittgenstein's philosophical remarks, while evidencing a characteristic rigor and a concern for that dimension of religious faith involving passion and personal appropriation, without the concepts of "grammar" and "forms of life" Holmer is hard-pressed to show what it is that makes religious belief distinctive. Where in his later writing he might challenge the notion of "assenting" as appropriate to what believers say and do, and instead speak of the "grammar of" belief and faith, in this early work he seems close to bifurcating the intellectual and affectional dimensions of belief. And again, in his desire to affirm the importance of personal appropriation—"becoming the possibility"—the question must be posed whether believers view their beliefs merely as "cognitive possibilities." It is to these and other related issues of "language and belief" that we will return in our discussion of Wittgenstein and Holmer's *The Grammar of Faith*.

3. Wittgenstein and Theology

According to Holmer, the over-arching perspective of Wittgenstein's philosophy—especially his later philosophy—is that many traditional

17. Ibid.
18. Ibid.
19. Ibid.

philosophical problems are, in fact, akin to "knots" or "bewitchments of our intelligence" caused by our use and understanding of language. Wittgenstein understands the primary task of philosophy as "untying" these knots and overcoming these bewitchments by paying close attention to the way in which we use language. As Holmer writes of Wittgenstein: "He did not seek any new information nor advance any kind of theory; but he looked very concertedly at the workings of our language—concepts, names, forms, rules, grammar, beliefs enshrined in our familiar expressions (meaning, sensation, thought, intend, feel, know, etc.)—in order to show how knots in our understanding developed."[20]

In Holmer's view, Wittgenstein's philosophy is best understood as a "treatment, even a therapy," not so much for the sake of forwarding new theories about traditional philosophical puzzles, but as a means of clearing away the obstacles to our understanding which create these puzzles. That is, primary attention is given not to proposing alternative theories for traditional philosophical issues, but to helping one to think clearly about these issues. This is not to say that Wittgenstein makes no positive contribution to philosophy (or, indirectly to theology) but that this contribution has more to do with a way of conceiving and practicing philosophical reflection than proposing a theory or system.

A similar perspective is found in Holmer's treatment of philosophical and theological issues where, once again, primary attention is focused on the "how" of philosophical and theological reflection rather than on forwarding new versions of its content. In both his writings and in his courses on philosophical theology at Yale Divinity School, Holmer employed his own version of Wittgenstein's way of conceiving and practicing philosophical reflection. As Holmer comments on his own work, he is seeking no novel understandings nor promoting a new theological system, but rather reflecting on how theology is done and the nature of the language we use. Like Wittgenstein, Holmer's intent is to re-connect theological language and reflection with the ordinary language and praxis of religious life. As we shall see, this means understanding theology and undertaking theological reflection within the context of prayer, worship and ethical reflection and action. For, as Holmer makes clear, it is within the concrete context of the life of faith that theology is properly grounded and theological reflection practiced.

20. Holmer, "Wittgenstein and Theology," 111.

Given the (apparent) influence of Wittgenstein's philosophy for contemporary philosophy and theology, the assumption is sometimes made that there is—or should be—a "Wittgensteinian theology." But as Holmer notes pointedly, he is not interested in promulgating such a theological school; rather he seeks to make use of Wittgenstein's particular way of *doing* philosophy as a means of untying the knots binding contemporary theological reflection. As he writes:

> We can suppose, too, that there might be "Wittgensteinian" theology some day. But I neither wish that nor need it, and I can only urge something more modest. If there is any point to reading Wittgenstein with the hope that he might help in one's theological difficulties, it might be because one could paraphrase him like this: Why is theology so complicated? It ought to be completely simple. Theology also unties those knots in our thinking which we have so unwisely put there; but its ways in untying must be as complicated as the knots are in tying. . . . The complexity of theology is not in its subject matter but rather in our knotted understanding and personality.[21]

As we have suggested, one of the characteristics of this "way" of doing philosophy is attention to language, to the way that language "works" in ordinary usage and to the features that contribute to its proper use in a given context. The addition of "personality" as an aspect of the knotted understanding afflicting contemporary theology suggests an important element of the context of language use; namely, the person using it. But Holmer's remarks also suggest a theme in his reading of Wittgenstein and an example of the reciprocal illumination provided by his seeing affinities between the work of Kierkegaard and Wittgenstein. For, in Holmer's view, the purpose of theology is to promote lived knowledge "of" God rather than merely proposing theories "about" God. In the context of examining Wittgenstein's significance for theology Holmer notes, "the point I wish to make is that often theology, like philosophy, is most disappointing when it is most obviously prosperous—when there is not only one theology but dozens of them. All one seems to get is points of view and not knowledge of God."[22]

Just as for Kierkegaard, for Holmer, logical and ethical concerns underlie the purposes of both philosophy and theology. In his reading of

21. Ibid., 112.
22. Ibid., 113.

Wittgenstein, Holmer sees these same concerns at work. For example, he notes the ethical underpinnings of Wittgenstein's *Tractatus*, and observes that this is the primary unifying feature of both Wittegenstein's early and later writings. As we shall see, it is this fundamental connection of logical and ethical concerns that Holmer discerns in Wittgenstein's thought that characterizes Holmer's own philosophical and theological reflection. This connection also indirectly suggests one use of Wittgenstein's philosophical reflections for theology. As Holmer understands the import of this perspective: "Instead of yielding to an easy skepticism, it seems to me that Wittgenstein's work urges more concern with details and closer scrutiny of the source of the theologian's puzzlement."[23] The subject of this "scrutiny," as we have noted, is the language used by believers and theologians in speaking about God. Holmer's primary interest, however, is with the ordinary language that believers use in the actual context of their religious life and practice. This means that the focus is on the connection between religious language and the context and use of this language in such activities as confession, prayer and worship. While the more specialized and conceptualized language of theology is of interest, it, too, is to be understood in light of its grounding in these religious practices. For it is precisely by attending to the ordinary uses of religious language and the forms of life with which they are connected that the knots in our understanding—particularly in more systematic theological reflection—will be untied. As Holmer argues, one of the demands of authentic theological reflection, in both a formal and a material sense, is "a greater congruence between our thoughts and our form of life.[24]

4. The Grammar of Belief

As one example of the use of Wittgenstein's perspective for philosophical and theological reflection, Holmer offers an analysis of the statements, "God is in Christ" and "Christians believe that God is in Christ." While on the surface these two statements appear similar, Holmer notes that they have quite distinct and different uses that determine their meaning. Whereas the former says something "theological in a first-person mode," the second, about what Christians believe, "is more like saying that a certain group of

23. Ibid.
24. Ibid., 115.

people have come to a theological view."[25] Holmer goes on to note: "Those two statements have quite different uses. If one asks about the truth of the second, we do quite distinctive things to ascertain what is what. Our measures and rules are different when we discuss whether or not there is "believing" than when we discuss whether God is in Christ."[26]

It is precisely the different "measures and rules" connected to the use of such statements that is essential to understanding their "grammar," in the sense of their ruled use in a particular language practice or "language game"; and it is by attending to and describing these that one is then in a position to say something about "the meaning" of the expression. As Holmer notes, Wittgenstein's analysis points beyond the surface similarities of such statements to the "depth grammar" and use of the statements within the complex of human practices and historic and cultural conventions, or what is termed a "form of life."

One question that is engaged by this kind of analysis is whether theology is a "kind of knowledge which can be stated independently from being believed?" While Wittgenstein does not answer this question directly, the force of his philosophical reflection on theological language is such that it directs us to look at the assumptions and subsequent confusions that are the result of apparent similarities in statements that have distinct and different uses. In this sense the "game of theology" is different than the "game" involved in determining what Christians believe. While the latter is open to factual investigation and empirical evidence, the former is not. As Holmer observes:

> Most "belief" looks like a transition into knowing, a temporary mind-state, vanquished by knowledge. We have a kind of standard forced upon us by the notion of being rational, namely, that we first find out whether it is so, then we, too, will believe. And our theologies tend in the direction of feeding this conception of rationality. However, this may well be the biggest knot in our understanding, the cramp in our thought, that produces some of the theologies and our misgivings about them when we get them.[27]

The issue at stake, then, is the grammar of the term "belief" as it is employed in different contexts. In order to untangle the knots in our understanding, attention must be paid to the actual use of statements beyond

25. Ibid.
26. Ibid.
27. Ibid., 117.

the fact that they may use this same term "belief." Whereas a determination of what Christians believe may be stated apart from such religious beliefs, there is no equivalent "knowing" in regard to the belief that God is in Christ; theology errs when it confuses these two different uses, and in so doing, both contributes to a misunderstanding of the nature of religious belief and misconstrues the basic character of theological reflection. As Holmer observes, "just why there might be a difference in 'belief' in respect to Christian teachings as over against other kinds of 'beliefs' (e.g., Goldbach's theorem, or 'that the chair will hold me') is lost to us by a very learned way of speaking."[28]

To overcome the confusions generated by the apparently propositional form of religious beliefs, theologians must learn once again to look at the actual context and content of such beliefs. As Holmer puts it: "To break out means that one looks at the teachings again, at the very homely details."[29] And going further in his description of the distinctive character of religious belief, Holmer writes: "There is something about Christian believing that makes it a constant struggle. One has to hold fast, almost in spite of the way the world is. One is tempted to say, in spite of the way that theology is, too. But surely something is wrong."[30]

It is in light of the implications of such close scrutiny of language evidenced in Wittgenstein's way of doing philosophy that Holmer proposes a different model for theology; as he writes: "It must be that part of the theological task is to free us from misleading analogies and the making of ideologies in Jesus' name. Maybe theologians also have to describe, not invent, and get clear on the limits of language for us once more."[31]

Getting clear on "the limits of language" might serve as a shorthand for Holmer's reformulation of the work of theology and its relation to philosophy. However, it is not so much that our language is limited as that our understanding of language is limited. For this reason the primary work of theology, like philosophy, is not to invent or propose new theories (or new languages), but rather, to undertake a careful "description" of religious language, beliefs and practices. This descriptive task is precisely what is lacking in the promulgation of a plethora of various "theologies of" which, in Holmer's polemic, plague the contemporary Christian theological scene.

28. Ibid.
29. Ibid., 118.
30. Ibid.
31. Ibid.

Again, as theology is called to attend to the lived context of the life of faith, to the practices that provide this context and thereby the setting for understanding the meaning of such beliefs, it is directed to the connection of belief and practice, faith and life. As Holmer writes: "About Wittgenstein's works we can say confidently that its technicalities are aimed at making us think right, but to think right requires that we live right. Few thinkers have been so technical and so disinterested as he was, but few thinkers have forced us to such honesty and such scrupulous self-understanding. . . . Maybe these are the requisites of theology as well as philosophy."[32]

It is this emphasis on the connection between "thinking right" and "living right" which characterizes both Holmer's use of Wittgenstein philosophy and his own constructive proposals for contemporary theological reflection. Perhaps more than any other contemporary philosophical theologian, Holmer emphasizes what he views to be a necessary correlation between language and life, theology and praxis. This is another place where Holmer sees a similarity between the writings of Kierkegaard and Wittgenstein. For example, in reflecting on Wittgenstein's fundamental understanding of philosophy and the role of personal involvement, Holmer writes about the development of a "capacity" for clear thinking in terms that might equally apply to Kierkegaard:

> He thought that Philosophy (hard thinking) could lead to the growth of the same capacity in the reader, if the reader would attend to his life and remarks with great care. Therefore, the distinctions he draws are not author-dependent in the usual way. They are also reader dependent. Unless we read him thus, we will miss much of the thrust of his pages. This is a kind of moral requisite demanded of the reader and I suspect makes Wittgenstein's later philosophy quite unpopular today. Philosophical reflection becomes particularly personal. It is not to be done by an assimilation of Wittgenstein's results. It is as though you have to *achieve* the capacity to make a distinction yourself or the distinction will not have any life at all.[33]

This last sentence may serve as a caveat for our own comments on Holmer's interpretation of Wittgenstein. For it must be said that, just as he is not interested in promoting a "Wittgensteinian" school of theology, Holmer's explicit remarks about Wittgenstein are most often occasional

---

32. Ibid.
33. Holmer, "Wittgenstein: 'Saying' and 'Showing,'" 223.

and stated within the context of addressing a particular philosophical or theological problem. As we have suggested, instead of discussing Wittgenstein directly, what Holmer does is to practice a way of philosophizing that is influenced by and shares similarities with Wittgenstein's thought. We will see a more extended example of this "way" of doing philosophy and its implications for theology in our examination of *The Grammar of Faith*. That said, there are some additional articles and manuscripts where Holmer's appropriation of Wittgenstein's thought is noted and where he comments on Wittgenstein's writings directly. It is to some of these that we will direct our attention in the balance of this chapter.

5. Saying and Showing

One place that Holmer sees the significance of Wittgenstein's philosophy for theology is in the important, even paradigmatic, logical distinction Wittgenstein draws between "saying" and "showing." In the *Tractatus* Wittgenstein writes: "There are some things that cannot be put into words. They *make themselves manifest*. They are what is mystical."[34] The seemingly enigmatic character of this expression is not lost on Holmer, but he argues that this is not an instance of Wittgenstein appealing to revelation or special intuition. Rather, according to Holmer, "the remarks he makes about the 'mystical' have force by virtue of logical disquisition, not by mystical apprehension."[35] It is the "logical" character of this distinction that Holmer finds of interest in this setting, and he views it as an insight carried through—albeit with modifications—into Wittgenstein's later writings. For this reason, Holmer sees a continuity between the early and later work of Wittgenstein and he is one of the few interpreters of Wittgenstein to note this fundamental similarity in perspective in both Wittgenstein's early and later writings. As Holmer observes: "One of the important and popular things to observe about Wittgenstein, for some years now, is the shift in view and kind of philosophizing which occurs after the *Tractatus*. But many of the major distinctions are in fact carried through into the later writings, and surely, a crucial one is the distinction between saying and showing."[36]

In the *Tractatus*, the import of the distinction between what language "shows" rather than "says" concerns the way in which the logical form of

34. Wittgenstein, *Tractatus*, 187; the sentence quoted is number 6.522.

35. Holmer, "Wittgenstein: 'Saying' and 'Showing,'" 222.

36. Ibid., 226.

propositions—as opposed to what propositions "say" directly—"shows" the way in which language "pictures the world." As Holmer articulates this distinction: "Propositions cannot represent logical form; it is mirrored in them, but finds its reflection or manifestation in language. Language cannot, as it were, 'say' the logical form. Rather, propositions 'show' the logical form, display it. What can be shown in this way, cannot be said."[37]

Holmer contends that Wittgenstein's view was, in a sense, "forced upon him" by his preoccupation with logical issues in the tradition of Frege, Russel and foundational questions in arithmetic. In light of his concern with what permits language to "picture the world," Wittgenstein concluded that there must be some coherence between propositions and states of affairs and came to the conclusion that language had embedded in it a "logical form." As Holmer points out, it was Wittgenstein's very preoccupation with logic that "led him to dissociate words and sentences altogether from the idiosyncracies of speakers, of situations, of mouths, of people."[38] But in Holmer's view, this way of understanding the distinction between saying and showing was an instance of "being misled by a picture." Speaking of the logical form of language in and of itself leaves out the crucial fact that it is people—not language itself—who say something in their use of language. Moreover, according to Holmer, Wittgenstein went even further in the *Tractatus*, "for the notion of 'logical form' is like an impersonal and radically independent factor in virtue of which language, 'per se,' in any mouth . . . gets hold of the world."[39] In this view, then, it is language itself that "pictures the world" apart from speakers.

The import of this notion for Wittgenstein is that the "logical form" built into language then looks to be "transcendental," and it is seen or displayed in such a way that this logical form belongs to the realm of "the mystical" and unsayable. But as Holmer notes, this distinction, at least as articulated in the *Tractatus*, is a curious one because by stating the distinction of what language shows rather than says it is as though Wittgenstein is transgressing the very limitation between "saying" and "showing" that he is noting.

As we have suggested, although there clearly is a shift in Wittgenstein's thinking when comparing the later writings with the *Tractatus*, according to Holmer, "the usefulness of the distinction between 'saying' and 'showing'

---

37. Ibid., 224.
38. Ibid., 225.
39. Ibid.

is not vitiated by the altered context and the new way of philosophizing that we find in the later works."[40] As Holmer understands it, even with the development of the notions of "language games" and "forms of life," the distinction between "saying" and "showing" remains "close to being fundamental"; and even as it appears in the *Tractatus*, "it looks to me as though it is indeed what Wittgenstein could call a grammatical remark. . . . It tells us something about why 'meaning' is not totally 'said,' about the essence of a range of expressions."[41]

For this reason, the distinction between saying and showing is appropriately continued in Wittgenstein's later philosophy. But where the earlier writings draw this distinction in reference to the way that language "shows" rather than "says" logical form, in the later writings Wittgenstein calls this a "grammatical" distinction: "For a grammatical distinction does not say what is unsayable, but it points the reader to saying and to showing, while not doing either."[42] The change that occurs between the earlier and later writings is that it is no longer a quality of language itself, language *qua* language, that is at issue; instead, in the later writings, the limit upon the capacity to say things is dependent upon "extra linguistic capacities" which contain the speaker, his situation and the context of his utterance. This is the different "whole" that Wittgenstein now has in mind when he reflects on the logical form or "fit" of language with the world: "Though Wittgenstein did, of course, mention 'logical form' in the *Tractatus*, he could admit no 'logical form' for the formation of true propositions about *that*, namely the 'logical form.' Neither was there a logical form for matters like God, 'the Good,' 'the Beautiful,' and so on. But with the *Investigations*, the orientation has changed. The language of the speakers, qualified in a rich variety of ways, becomes a matter for logical inquiry."[43]

In the *Investigations* Wittgenstein is no longer abstracting language from speakers, situations and actual use, and it is this change, according to Holmer, that allows him to do justice to the earlier distinction. As Holmer

40. Ibid., 226.

41. Ibid.

42. Ibid., 224. Even in noting this change, however, Holmer reiterates his perspective on the use of Wittgenstein's philosophy as proposing not a theory but rather an occasion for the individual to look for him or herself. As he writes: "So the 'distinction' Wittgenstein makes between saying and showing is, even if grammatical, also an occasion for seeing something for yourself. It is not a substitute for seeing what is manifest. Seeing is a capacity and can only be done by people, not by sayings" (ibid.).

43. Ibid., 228.

puts it: "Now the possibility, the logical space, is made by speakers of the language in their social habits, and in the forms of activity and intention in which they participate."[44]

Within the context of this change there still remain some things that cannot be said directly but must be shown. As an example, Holmer looks at the expression "there is a world." Within the realm of physics, for example, this may appear to be a basic or fundamental proposition underlying the things that physicists do and seems analogous with such ordinary statements as "there is a table," or "there is a chair." However, the expression, "there is a world" is not what one would normally call a remark in physics, and the assumption of an analogy with the earlier statements is a misleading one. As Holmer puts it, the "problem lies in attempting to put this into words" insofar as "the physicists alleged certainty about the existence of the world becomes a philosophical problem only when one attempts to state it *as* a proposition."[45] In this case, like the earlier distinction between "saying" and "showing," the certainty of the existence of the world cannot be stated directly in a proposition but is rather "shown" in what physicists do and say. It is the activity of physicists that serves as a ground for their convictions about the world rather than any explicit belief. This is not to say that we become certain there is a world by having physicists show us, because their activities show their certainty in the same way that "by learning to live with tables and chairs, and with a range of familiar activities and things, we all become certain of there being a world."[46] As Holmer presents Wittgenstein's perspective, there is no special learning about "world" and its existence; the role of philosophy consists rather in a kind of "grammatical remark" that reminds us that some things are said and others things only shown.

For Holmer, the fundamental import of Wittgenstein's expressions about "language games" and "forms of life," is that language is understood to be "bound up with a game one is playing and with the very form and character that one's whole life acquires."[47] As Wittgenstein states it in his *On Certainty*: "My life shows that I know or am certain that there is a chair over there, or a door and so on—I tell a friend, e.g., 'Take that chair over there,' 'Shut the door,' etc. etc."[48]

44. Ibid.
45. Ibid., 229.
46. Ibid.
47. Ibid.
48. Wittgenstein, *On Certainty*, 2.

Holmer notes that Wittgenstein said similar things about "meaning" that fit within the "saying and showing" distinction as well. He observes that while "it is clear enough that Wittgenstein did not want to write a theory of meaning," a more subtle point is "the fact that the meaning of a sentence is not something that can be said, that can be written out, in another sentence."[49] In Holmer's view, this grammatical remark has a special relevance to the long practice of theologians who presume to state "the meaning" of the figurative or parabolic language of religion in specialized theological concepts. As we will see in Holmer's *The Grammar of Faith*, this is one of the fundamental problems that Holmer deals with by an application of Wittgenstein's way of philosophizing.

Briefly stated, the point of contention is that, for Wittgenstein, meaning is not something existing outside a given language use but rather, as Holmer summarizes this position, "once one understands how a word fits into the discourse then, by and large, one already has the meaning of the word."[50] What it means to understand a word is to know its place within a particular language use or "game." Rather than stating the meaning in an additional assertion—or by translation into another conceptuality—"to be able to place the word, where it makes an appropriate difference and does a job, is to show by your behavior that a word has meaning."[51] Again, for Holmer, this is not a "theory of meaning," but rather a "grammatical remark," a descriptive rendering of what is the case.

Holmer perceives here another permutation of the "saying and showing" distinction and extends this to touch on what he terms the "ethical" import of Wittgenstein's grammatical and logical descriptions. He notes that like the meaning of a word, the meaning of life "is also such that men can not say in what it consists," because "it does not consist in anything that is part of the tissue of facts, that is sayable." He goes on to note this theme in Wittgenstein's early and later writings:

> This is a strong theme in the *Tractatus* (6.521), in his letters, and in the *Notebooks* (June, July, August, 1916) to the effect that even those men to whom long doubt had finally yielded a clear sense and meaning of life, could not say what made up that sense. This was not due to a vocabulary deficiency. I think that there is a deep but somewhat difficult and obscure connection between

49. Holmer, "Wittgenstein: 'Saying' and 'Showing,'" 231.
50. Ibid.
51. Ibid.

> Wittgenstein's earlier reflections and the fact that sense and mean-
> ing are still not sayable, even for our working language, in his later
> pages. For both early and late it is a mistake to say that meaning
> consists in something, as if it lay within the facts (*Tractatus*) or
> were an activity in whole or in part consisting in saying, in utter-
> ances, of meanings (*Zettel*, nos. 16 and 19).[52]

As we will attempt to show in our next chapter, what Holmer calls
this "deep and obscure connection" in Wittgenstein's thought between what
can be said and what cannot serves as a catalyst for his own reflections
on the "meaning" of religious beliefs and how this meaning is "shown" in
one's life. In a similar way, we might posit that reflecting on this issue as it
appears in Wittgenstein's writings influences both Holmer's understanding
of the limitations of theology and his reflections on what it means to "make
sense" with one's life. Here the still indirect, but more explicitly religious
perspective that Kierkegaard brings to bear on these issues helps Holmer to
articulate his "morphology of the life of Christian belief," both what cannot
be said and what must be said.

In this context Holmer employs Wittgenstein's distinctions and remarks to reflect on the grammar of various "psychological verbs," such as
"knowing," "understanding," "hoping," "intending," and "wanting." Holmer
notes that Wittgenstein argued that it is a mistake to view these verbs as
some kind of internal activity or hidden process. As an example, Holmer
looks at the concept "wanting," observing that it does not consist in an inward activity that is then externalized in words, but rather having a want is
more like having an orientation: "It is a way that a person disposes himself
towards people, events, his future, his abilities, his expectations."[53] And this,
too, is "shown" in the person's behavior, although not in a singular act, but
in the long-term disposition and orientation of a person's life. It is not that
wants are not capable of being verbalized in words, but rather, as Holmer
puts it, that a verbalization alone does not suffice to show it. As Holmer
writes:

> For persons who do not know what they want, there is no inquiry
> by which to find out, certainly no technique of introspecting; for
> a want is not there to be introspected. It has to be formed, usually
> slowly and with effort. Our lives are also spent in learning to want,
> to want significantly and steadily. Thus "saying" our want here is

52. Ibid., 232.
53. Ibid., 233.

dependent upon the rest of our life acquiring significant transparency and shape, so that it can be said to have any form. A want, a life-long want, does, of course, form a life. It is off of a well-formed life, and only such a life, even our own, that a want can be read at all.[54]

Once again, here something nonlinguistic serves to show us what we mean. For unless a person's form of life bears out what he says he wants, the saying counts for little. And while there may be short-term wants that seem more readily stateable in words, even in these cases, what one wants is still "shown." In the case of longer-term wants Holmer sees this intensified to the point of becoming not only a logical but a life issue: "More encompassing wants are even more difficult to 'say.' This, what one has wanted is the sort of thing that cannot be stated since one's life will show that instead. It will show itself. Learning what one ought and can want is a good part of what makes a life human and also manifest. Not to have any great want is not to have lived as a man."[55]

Holmer notes another "troublesome matter" that Wittgenstein links to the "showing and saying" issue, commenting that "his remarks about happiness are at once cryptic and enigmatical, but also exceedingly attractive." In answer to the question, "How does happiness manifest itself, if it cannot be said?" Wittgenstein responds that this is shown in a variety of ways such as "living fearlessly, even in the face of death," and "living in the present, not being tortured by the past or prospects of the future." But it is Wittgenstein's remark that a happy man is one who is "fulfilling his existence, but without having to acknowledge a purpose," no longer needing "to have any purpose, that is to say, who is content," that is most suggestive to Holmer.[56] For he reads Wittgenstein as saying that happiness is not something that can be factually described but is instead manifest "in the entire world being a different one for the happy man than for the unhappy one."[57] The "world" here is not factually different, for there is no one thing to point to or state in empirical terms. It is not something one can prove or for which one can provide a map; and yet for all that, it is a place one can live. As Holmer puts it: "When the world and men thus are not in enmity, when contentment

---

54. Ibid.

55. Ibid., 234.

56. Wittgenstein, *Notebooks*, 72–73, quoted in Holmer, "Wittgenstein: 'Saying' and 'Showing,'" 234.

57. Ibid., 234.

and peace are exemplified, when the dogged and terrifying problems about the existence of God about the good, about the meaning of life are, not answered, but vanquished altogether, then happiness shines forth."[58]

Noting the similarity in Wittgenstein's remarks about philosophy being successful when one can stop doing philosophy, Holmer emphasizes the proviso that both cases presuppose that one has been genuinely concerned with these important issues, that one has struggled with them and through arduous and serious engagement has come to this new understanding. Happiness in this sense, along with logical clarity, is a kind of achievement for which there are no shortcuts.

It is for these reasons that Holmer finds Wittgenstein's early remarks on "saying and showing" and it's connection with his later notion of "form of life" so significant. For there is something very subtle and profound at work in Holmer's reading of Wittgenstein. He senses both the logical import, the analytic significance of Wittgenstein's remarks, and he practices a similar discipline; and yet, he perceives the wider implications of these remarks and this way of philosophizing for a whole host of issues. It is by means of a rigorous and insightful use of Wittgenstein's descriptive grammatical analysis that Holmer moves on to the deeper, human significance of the concepts under analysis. It is this latter extension of Wittgenstein's way of doing philosophy that marks Holmer as an especially profound interpreter of Wittgenstein, and more importantly, that characterizes Holmer's own contribution to philosophy. For here no abstract system is proposed nor a new metaphysics, but instead a careful description of the workings of ordinary language within the activities of human life. And it precisely by this close attention to what people say and do with words and beyond words that Holmer touches on the most fundamental and enduring issues of human life.

6. Language and Theology

The so-called "problem of religious language" with which we began this chapter has been a perennial concern of philosophical and theological reflection and both the perception of the issue and the responses to it have a wide variety of permutations. As a way of concluding our discussion of Holmer's appropriation and interpretation of Wittgenstein's philosophy we will examine another treatment of this issue by Holmer under the title of

58. Ibid., 234–35.

"Language and Theology," first published in 1965."[59] Through an application of insights culled from Wittgenstein's reflections on language Holmer here offers a careful analysis of both the alleged "problem" and some of the responses to it.

One of the ways that the "crisis" of religious language is sometimes portrayed, according to Holmer, is that the language of theology—or better, the language of faith—as presented in Scripture, creeds, and the discourse of believers is no longer viable. What is contended is that these older, vernacular forms of speech no longer express what they were intended to express, that although people may understand the words, they no longer comprehend the meanings. One response to this dilemma on the part of theologians has been to argue the need for new vocabularies and conceptualities in which to express the meanings of the more ancient and now archaic language forms.

As Holmer views it, what is implied here, and sometimes even stated directly, is that the words used are merely symbols for thoughts and ideas— for the meanings, if you will—and therefore they may be replaced by other, more modern and adequate symbols. On the one hand, although Holmer does not deny that languages change, he argues that these changes are not such to make ordinary religious language obsolete or the meanings of its concepts obscure. And, more importantly, it is what he terms a "mentalist" or "spiritualized" picture of "meaning" that is the fundamental issue at stake. For as Holmer sees it: "A kind of spiritualization of language takes place among us, and most of that finds its fruition in a notion that the realm of meaning is mentalistic, inside of our heads, and finally the sort of place or region to which a person has only his private and privileged access."[60]

In Holmer's view, a familiar dichotomy—a "misleading picture," in Wittgenstein's terms—is at work here, where words are taken to be the physical (and almost arbitrary) representations of what are "mental," perhaps even pre-linguistic, meanings. In this view, it is as though one first has thoughts and ideas and subsequently translates them into the words of speech or writing. This "dogma," in Holmer's terms, "causes us to think that meanings are kinds of events, objects, persons, or things lying behind language and for which language is supposed to stand. But then all language,

---

59. Holmer, "Language and Theology," first published in *Harvard Theological Review*. We will cite the revised version of this essay that appears in *The Grammar of Faith*.

60. Holmer, "Language and Theology," in *Grammar of Faith*, 119. This sentence does not appear in the original article.

verbal and written, is a symbolic activity."[61] Holmer further characterizes this view as "a piece of metaphysics, not a matter of common sense or scientific description." For if "to mean" was this kind of private, internalized activity, there would be no public or ruled access to meaning, and the meanings attached to words could be whatever an individual chose them to be. A straightforward empirical look at how people use language shows this is simply not how things are.

Holmer notes—à la Wittgenstein—that "words do nothing by themselves. They neither refer or fail to refer."[62] Rather, it is people who do the referring and use words to do so. This observation suggests that the "meaning-complexes" that we call concepts and use to refer are not separate entities lying behind our words but are more adequately described as "realized capacities," powers or abilities "accumulated in the life history of an individual." Concepts function as the "organization of emotions, feelings, references and a wide variety of thought-contents which our behavior and its contexts require."[63] Holmer argues that there is no special realm of concepts, apart from words, for concepts are among the things that words express when people use them in regularly recognized ways, in keeping with the conventions of the language. According to Holmer, conceptual meaning "is made by the way our ordinary language works."[64] In opposition to what he has termed a metaphysical view of language, and despite the prevalence of the idea in theological circles, Holmer contends that there is no special conceptual language that might better serve to accomplish what we do in ordinary language.

As we have seen, then, informed by the perspectives Wittgenstein brings to bear on some of these same issues, Holmer views both "the problem of religious language" and the theological penchant for new theological systems and conceptualities as based largely on a mistaken view of language. There is no single philosophy of language in the sense of a single explanation of how meanings are bestowed (not even, we should note, Wittgenstein's often misunderstood and misused remarks about the connection of meaning and use), nor a conceptual scheme standing behind language awaiting discovery. It is not that concepts cannot be studied or

---

61. Ibid., 118.

62. Holmer, "Language and Theology," in *Grammar of Faith*, 121. The sentence does not appear in the original article.

63. Ibid.

64. Ibid., 122.

discussed but that such second-order reflection is not what imparts meaning to them. Instead, as Wittgenstein noted, meanings are "part of the situation in which language is used, where speaker and writer talk to secure the listener's and reader's responses."[65] It is for this reason that Holmer turns his attention to the ordinary uses of religious language, the contexts in which they occur and the practices with which they are associated. As Holmer puts it: "I am contending, instead, that attention be paid to the actual workings of the speech-forms. When these are put to work in their appropriate contexts, then the meanings simply occur. Therefore it is a mistake to treat metaphysics and theology as though they actually supplied meanings to more ordinary religious discourse."[66]

Thus, the appropriate response to the alleged demise of religious language, according to Holmer, is not to offer new conceptual systems into which vernacular religious language must be translated but "to suggest the 'learning how' and all that that involves in the religious life" including the use of religious language in its many forms. For where there are these uses, where they are practiced and inculcated, religious words and concepts have meaning. Concepts like "God," "sin," "grace," and "salvation," are achievements developed in the context of the struggle of faith and have their meaning therein.

What this means for Holmer is that there is no shortcut to restoring meaning to religious language, no way save the "long pull of educating the human spirit as to what religion is."[67] The task of the theologian is not, therefore, to invent additional artificial linguistic contexts or meanings, but rather to attend to religious concepts and their logic and grammar within the life and practices of religious faith. Then the task of the theologian "would be a kind of description of what is already achieved rather than an attempt to provide what's missing."[68] For, as Holmer puts it, when words lose their meaning, it is not the words that are at fault, but the people using them, and religious words lose their meaning "when nothing follows their usage, when the individual does not seem to know anything about the matters to which they refer and the way of life in which they were born."[69] To

65. Ibid., 127.
66. Ibid., 130.
67. Ibid., 131.
68. Ibid., 131–32.
69. Ibid., 135.

teach this, to describe the connection of religious concepts, their context and the form of life in keeping with them, is the theologian's task.

As we will suggest, it is to this "descriptive" task that Holmer turns in his own work. It is, as he understands it, a different way of conceiving the work of theology than that of system-building or providing meanings. It is to return to the ordinary and nontechnical language uses of the Bible, the liturgy and hymns, "the language of fishermen, tax collectors and tentmakers"; for it is this "primitive way of speaking," this "ordinary language of ordinary believers," which provides the meaning of more technical theological discourse and not the other way around.[70]

According to Holmer, then, the point of "linguistic analysis," as applied to theology, is not a better way—now analytic instead of speculative—to do the same thing; indeed, as he notes: "Wittgenstein's reflections on these matter are more in the direction of liquidating philosophy as the science of meanings than of inventing one more permutation of methods to provide them."[71] Instead, it is to do a new thing. It is to reflect on "the grammar of faith." It is to Holmer's further reflections on these matters in his *The Grammar of Faith* that we will now turn.

70. Ibid., 132.
71. Ibid.

3

The Grammar of Faith

1. Introduction

> Theology is that discipline in which the believers declare what the
> facts are, what the hopes, fears and loves are, what the beliefs are,
> for those who find God in Christ Jesus.[1]

IN HIS PREFACE TO *The Grammar of Faith* Paul Holmer begins by noting the
use of the word "grammar" in his title. Although he acknowledges his debt
to Karl Pearson's *The Grammar of Science* for its use as a term describing
a "kind of schematic sense" and to John Henry Newman's proposal in *The
Grammar of Assent* that "assenting" is deeply ruled, it is primarily Ludwig
Wittgenstein's use of the term in his *Philosophical Investigations* which gave
"a new impetus and a more careful set of considerations to go with the
expression." As Holmer goes on to note: "A leading thought of his book
suggests that quite primitive instances of the language of faith and the life of
faithful believers answer to one another. Both belong to a single grammar."[2]
It is this connection of the language of faith and the life of faithfulness,
what he terms "this single grammar," that Holmer seeks to explore in *The
Grammar of Faith*.

The fundamentally polemical perspective underlying this collection
of essays is immediately apparent when Holmer says that these writings
are a response to what he terms the "scandal" of contemporary academic

1. Holmer, *Grammar of Faith*, 8–9.
2. Ibid., ix.

theology, which he characterizes as one of "competing 'isms,' contradictions, meta-views," an intellectual jumble of speculation and "senseless system-mongering." Beyond the lack of intellectual rigor and logical precision that this plethora of competing theological systems evidences, Holmer argues that they also misrepresent "the actual life of Christian belief and morals" while producing nothing so much as a "pervasive religious skepticism."[3] This thoroughgoing and biting critique of what he assesses to be "loosely articulated schemes of thought" with "profound logical flaws" where "the pseudo-learning of our day" has made "believing in God and in Jesus Christ (not only in doctrines about God or in Christologies)" implausible, clearly reflects something of the frustrations of Holmer's experience in an academic environment that fostered this situation.

Although he is direct in acknowledging the polemical orientation of his argumentation, Holmer nonetheless suggests that his intent in *The Grammar of Faith* is constructive as well, "in the direction of defining theology anew," by "providing the logic of theology."[4] But even as he forwards his constructive proposal to present "another morphology of the life of Christian belief," he argues that it is "a logic and a grammar that we miss often because of a monstrous illusion fostered by a pattern of thought and speech, wherein objectivity, fact, meaning, truth, and even faith are advertised but never delivered."[5] Our examination of *The Grammar of Faith* is undertaken with the purpose of analyzing both Holmer's polemic and his constructive proposals for theology.

2. What Theology Is and Does

In the first essay, "What Theology Is and Does," Holmer begins by noting that theology is "interpretation." But he quickly goes on to observe that significantly more needs to be added to this definition, namely, one must determine precisely what it is that theology interprets and for what purpose. There is, for example, a mode of interpretation that focuses attention on an historical accounting where the primary concern is with the context, historical and social, of the various writings of the Bible. But as Holmer argues, "it is one kind of game in which the telling of the story is done only

3. Ibid., x.
4. Ibid., 4.
5. Ibid., x.

to fill out the account of Middle Eastern history, and quite another to tell it in order to make the reader a part of a community of faith."[6]

It is, of course, this latter mode that Holmer has in mind when he goes on to state his understanding of the purpose of theological interpretation: "But when I tell the story, maybe the same story even down to the details, so that one will emulate the ancient's courage, live their virtues, eschew their vices, find their law, and seek their God with might and finesse of spirit, then I am doing something quite different. Another game is being played."[7] Although Holmer uses the term "interpretation," he appears intent on distinguishing his meaning from that of, for example, Rudolph Bultmann's existentalist interpretation or what was termed the "new hermeneutic," when he notes, "nothing esoteric or rare is supposed here by the word *interpretation*," and "it is not being supposed that 'interpretation' is the only way to get 'meaning' or that 'interpreting' is a subtle intellectual necessity to get some kind of scheme going on otherwise neutral facts."[8] As Holmer views it, the kind of interpretation that is central to theology is not simply the ordering of supposedly "neutral facts" for the sake of arriving at their meaning. Indeed, Holmer argues that there are no neutral facts; the popular conception that science, as opposed to the humanities, is only about the facts and that the latter alone commerce in interpretation is characterized as "a dual conviction, unremittingly confused and false."[9] Although theology may indeed be rightly described as interpretation it is wrong to contrast this with a view of historical studies as the supposedly objective study of facts apart from interpretation. Suggesting the influence of Wittgenstein's later writings, Holmer argues: "The point is that both of these are like games in one respect—namely, that therein we can play the field according to the rules. But there is no subgame basic to all the rest. There are, instead, interpretations: one way that is theological, where everything is referred to God and the Godly life; another way that is historical, where another set of concerns about antecedents and consequences, causes and effects, and how 'this' became 'that' are entertained."[10]

6. Ibid., 5.

7. Ibid.

8. Ibid.

9. Ibid.

10. Ibid., 6. Holmer's use of the term "game" here suggests both Wittgenstein's use of the concept "game" as an example of a term which in its various uses shares not a common core meaning but rather a "family resemblance," and his notion of "language games."

Holmer goes on to contend that it is the kind of interpretation called "historical studies" that is, in fact, the newer "game"; it yields not the primary or fundamental interpretation but instead simply one kind of understanding, namely, "historical understanding." Just as there are no bare facts there is no such thing as "the" understanding which theology supposedly articulates by "explaining" the primary sources of the faith. Instead, as Holmer argues, there are "historical facts and theological facts . . . an historical understanding of the Scriptures and a theological understanding of those same pages."[11] The difference between the two involves the concerns that one brings to the sources and the purpose toward which one is directed.

Although this may be seen as a point of argument, Holmer's primary observation here is presented simply as a description noting the differing logics at work in historical as opposed to theological interpretation. Where Holmer suggests a critique of present theological assumptions is when he goes on to argue that theological interpretation does not necessarily require a historical-critical perspective. For example, in reading the New Testament in order to understand its deepest religious themes, he writes, "it is far more important than most historical material to learn to hunger and thirst for righteousness, to learn to love a neighbor, and to achieve a high degree of self-concern."[12] Particularly in an academic context of biblical studies where historical interpretation is presumed to be both primary and essential, Holmer's challenge here is a radical one. Indeed, if the genuinely theological reading of scripture is one that focuses on the personal address of scripture and sees its fundamental concern as the qualification of personal self-understanding, then historical interpretation may not only be unnecessary but, if assumed to be primary, becomes a barrier to comprehension of the meaning of the biblical text. Although this does not negate the significance of the concerns and conclusions of historical research, it does not confuse these concerns, nor make them antecedent to, specifically theological interests.

Holmer goes on to state more fully what his view of theology is when he writes: "Theology is that discipline in which the believers declare what the facts are, what the hopes, fears and loves are, what the beliefs are, for those who find God in Christ Jesus."[13] In this understanding theology is the form—or forms—of thought that believers share in their understand-

11. Ibid., 8.
12. Ibid., 9.
13. Ibid., 8–9.

ing of themselves, God and the everyday world. This does not mean that theological interpretation is either subjective or episodic because for Holmer it is the shared understanding, enduring over time and place that is of central concern in theological studies. And it is precisely the enduring characteristics of this understanding of the essentials of the faith, and the concomitant concern of personal appropriation of these essentials, which defines the specifically theological, as opposed to historical, interpretation. As Holmer states it again, "Theology is that game which we must play if we are to refer our lives to God."[14]

As we touched upon in the introduction to this chapter, in his polemic against some characteristics of modern academic theology Holmer disputes what he sees as an unfounded presupposition that theology needs to be modernized or made relevant by a philosophical ideology currently in vogue. Among those he specifically cites are process and the "neo-theologies" of "hope," "liberation," "minorities," and "women." As he writes: "Besides having a very short life, these 'theologies' often prove to be thinly disguised apologies for causes which hardly need such a rationale. Whatever their momentary appeal, such theologies do very little by way of recommending Christianity; instead they recommend causes that do not usually need such extraneous supports anyway."[15]

It is this aspect of Holmer's polemical tone that has contributed to the perception that his views are fundamentally conservative and even reactionary. Yet if one attends closely to his critique, it is not the substance of these causes that he repudiates but rather the need for theology directly to incorporate such views in its interpretive work. It is precisely because authentic Christian theology has direct linkage to the concepts of hope, of liberation, and equality before God, among others, that it does not need explicitly to be linked to a particular cause or issue. In a related critique, it is Holmer's contention that the very attempt to make Christianity attractive to modern ears in this way may lead to a misrepresentation of the faith: "A theology that is immediately attractive is often a poor introduction to the Christian life and thought. One must never entertain, therefore, a picture of a Christian theology as a net of causes and reasons, an intellectual proposal, which by constant assimilation of novelties, by continual adaptation to new circumstances, will reclaim the masses by its sweet reasonableness."[16]

14. Ibid., 9.
15. Ibid., 10.
16. Ibid., 11.

Holmer's charge against what he terms "journalistic theology" is that it too easily loses its "Godly and supernatural content" and "its timeless and eternal subject matter."[17] Rather than clothing popular causes and contemporary issues in the language of faith, the proper ordering of the task of theology is to view these causes and ideas in relation to God and God's dealings with humanity. As Holmer notes: "It is in this way that Christianity stays always relevant, for nothing is outside of God's purview and domain."[18]

Holmer goes on to observe that this critique of theology becoming subservient to contemporary intellectual fashions does not thereby mean that theological formulations are timeless; rather the work of the theologian is to mediate between the two foci of "the varying passions of men and the abiding verities of God."[19] What Holmer proposes is a theology done "in the vernacular," in "the diction of the common life," rather than language that is archaic, esoteric or excessively learned. It is precisely because the concerns of theology are not specialized or overtly "academic" but personal and ordinary, that they direct attention to an articulation of the faith in the vernacular.

Holmer then proceeds to articulate what it actually means to do theology in the vernacular. This is, in fact, a significant part of the task of preaching, as Holmer asks, "For what is else is good preaching but vernacular theology?"[20] For theology to be vernacular does not mean that theology must adopt the "argot of the age;" indeed, in its polemical function, the work of theological reflection is to tell us "what Christianity is and what and who God and we are," precisely in order to relate it to those aspects of contemporary self-understanding which they challenge and call into question. Holmer argues that many beliefs and assumptions of our age regarding human progress or "the idea that there is a new and general enlightenment and that human welfare can be secured by politics and science," do not provide a new point of departure or content for theological thinking, but rather, "must theology be done by people who, scientifically trained and technically skilled though they may be, must always be students of both Scripture and church teachings, on the one hand, and the

17. Ibid.
18. Ibid., 12.
19. Ibid., 13.
20. Ibid., 14.

passions of the human heart, on the other."[21] These concerns and passions, as Holmer describes them, "the deep and long-standing enthusiasm for justice, for health, for everlasting life, for peace, for love, for understanding, for safety"—are the common subject matter of political systems and scientific schemes that promise progress, but "unless a human heart can be addressed," the long term aim of theology will not be met.

For this reason what Holmer means by the "ordinary language of faith" is neither the language of the academy, contemporary science nor "pop psychology," but instead what he forwards in his own homiletical rhetoric as "that residual language, that common diction, within which we all understand and describe the bitterness of grief, the anguish of hopelessness, the fate of the defeated, the cries of the weary, the hurt feelings of the neglected, and the elation of the victor."[22] What matters here is not speaking in the language and parlance of the learned but speaking simply and from the heart.

3. Theology as Pedagogy and Polemic

In the second chapter of *The Grammar of Faith* Holmer continues his critique and forwards his constructive proposals concerning the nature and task of theology. It is here that he explicitly introduces his understanding and use of Wittgenstein's notion that theology may be construed as the grammar of faith.[23] What Holmer means by "grammar" here is the underlying and imbedded rules for making sense in and with language. Although learning grammar may be undertaken as a subject matter in itself, the real significance of grammar is not speaking about the grammar itself but acquiring the mastery of a language where our knowledge of grammar

---

21. Ibid., 15.

22. Ibid., 15–16.

23. In a footnote, Holmer presents a brief summary of his understanding of Wittgenstein's significance: "His thought is so different from most because he called a halt to the making of ideologies in the name of philosophy. He did not write a new philosophy—if one means by that a new metaphysics or a new morals or a new philosophy of religion. Instead, he tried to get clear all kinds of elementary things, like the differences between names and concepts, and activities and capacities like 'intending,' 'thinking,' and 'believing'—matters that have produced ideologies in the past but that he thought we had not gotten clear enough about. So his writings are full of brief but very powerful investigations of this and that—often matters that are almost commonplace. But he treats them with a difference" (17 n. 1).

informs all that we say and write. In learning the grammar our goal is not to speak about the rules of the language directly but rather to speak the language according to its rules and practices.

Holmer suggests that there is a similarity between the learning and use of grammar and the learning and use of logic. Once again, in the teaching of logic forms and rules can be isolated and taught in an abstract way; however, the real intent is not for one explicitly to recall the rules of logic but rather to become logical in their thinking and speaking. As Holmer puts it: "What starts out being a subject matter that we teach, say grammar or logic, becomes eventually no longer a separate subject matter at all, but instead a practice, a 'how', by which one does his talking and writing and thinking."[24] What this further suggests is that although one may learn the rules of grammar or logic separately, as these rules are embedded in the ordinary concourse of speech and practice, we also learn them from the practices themselves. Indeed, the more competent we become in the practices the less overt our knowledge of the rules is or needs to be.

It is a similar relation of rules and practices that Holmer sees as operative in the realm of theology. Although it, too, may be learned as a distinct subject matter, like grammar, theology is not an end in itself:

> But there is the additional difference about theology, though it is like grammar is some respects, namely, in not being the aim and intent of belief and the substance in and of itself (i.e., in not being the end but the means), still it is the declaration of the essence of Christianity. In so far as Christianity can be 'said' at all, theology and Scripture say it. But what is therein said, be it the words of eternal life, be it creeds, or be it the words of Jesus Himself, we must note that like grammar and logic, their aim is not that we repeat the words. Theology also must be absorbed, and when it is, the hearer is supposed to become Godly.[25]

Holmer's point is that, as in the case with grammar and logic, the real appropriation of theology is seen not in speaking about theology as a distinct subject matter, but rather in thinking and acting theologically; where theology differs from grammar and logic is in its having a content—namely, faith in God—but the nature of this content is such that, like grammar and logic, it is not the rules or logic, per se, but the appropriate practices of faith that matter.

24. Ibid., 18.
25. Ibid., 19.

Another way in which theology is akin to grammar is that we do not simply make up the rules as we go along. Like grammar, theology is a set of criteria and law-like remarks that describe how people think when they are making sense. But whereas these rules operate as prescriptions for one first learning the language, with mastery of the practices, the rules become part of the way we believe and act. And in a larger sense theology is also dependent upon a consensus of belief and practice, in the case of Christian theology, that of Jesus and the apostles, of Scripture and the lives of those whose story it tells. As Holmer goes on to state: "Theology answers the question—what is Christianity? But it tells us the answer by giving us the order and priorities, the structure and morphology, of the Christian faith. It does this by placing big words like 'man,' 'God,' 'Jesus,' 'world,' in such a sequence and context that their use becomes ruled for us."[26]

It is, according to Holmer, in the same way that a grammarian discovers the rules of language that we learn about God. That is, it is not "by seeking God through the cracks in the universe" nor by inventing a "finer conceptual net," but rather by attending carefully to "our common working speech." It is precisely in what we access to already—Scripture, the creeds, and the Christian tradition—that one comes to understand, for example, "what the Christian concept of God includes and excludes."[27] It is for this reason that theological proficiency—in its primary sense—is not dependent upon specialized academic training or scholarly approaches.

In its similarity to grammar, in focusing on the criteria or rules, what theology makes possible is "hearing the rules of the game in explicit fashion rather than having to read them off the game itself."[28] Although this is never a substitute for the practices of prayer, worship and service, theology does provide a kind of abridgement that allows a more immediate access to the rules embedded within these practices of faith. It is in this sense that theology may serve as a kind of shorthand for the proper use of theological concepts. In Holmer's view, this is the way, for example, that Paul's admonitions to the early church or Luther's reflections on Scripture work within the context of the life of faith.

Holmer goes on to suggest a still larger meaning of theology as grammar when he writes: "This theology of which I speak is infinitely more glorious, though, than the term 'grammar' might suggest. For theology does

26. Ibid., 20.

27. Ibid., 21.

28. Ibid., 22.

not parse verbs, arrange thoughts, and conjugate sentences. Its matter is finally the whole of human life itself. Insofar as it is grammar, it is more like the teaching that leads to a truly successful, deeply satisfactory, even blessed and happy life."[29] Because of the particular nature of the subject matter and therefore the content of theology, in the perspectives it provides on the world, God, and human nature, it proposes a kind of "shaping of human destiny." As we will discuss at a later point, it is this larger meaning of theology as a kind of grammar of life in a prescriptive as well as a descriptive sense that leads D. Z. Phillips to characterize Holmer as being both a grammarian and a "guardian" of the faith.

The continuing work of theological reflection is, in this view, not the promulgation of alternate readings of Scripture in keeping with the sensibilities of each new age nor the proposition of novel theories, but rather "learning to extend the rules, the order, the morphology, of Godliness over the ever-changing circumstances" of human history.[30] The constructive work of the theologian is, according to Holmer, "the responsibility of continually showing that God's grammar is sufficiently flexible to take in the novelties of our changing life."[31] And as Holmer goes on to note, it is the articulation of "sameness in differences, likeness in change," that is, the unchanging character of God's will in different circumstances, which is both the Gospel's enduring theme and the ongoing challenge to the theologian.

It is because it involves an application of the gospel to changing circumstances that the interpretive work of the theologian needs to be couched, as we noted earlier, "in the vernacular." As Holmer presents it, theology is not primarily a compendium or sum of truths; rather, its form is often occasional and even "accidental." And where it may begin in what Holmer terms the "about" mood, it must "always move towards a present-tense, first-person mood."[32] That is, although theology may be taught in a third-person mood—as a language "about" God—its proper use requires that it becomes one's own language "of" faith. It is this move to the language of faith rather than simply teachings about faith that constitutes the "vernacular" in Holmer's usage and characterizes the form of personal appropriation that is essential to genuine knowledge of God: "Otherwise," as

29. Ibid.
30. Ibid., 23.
31. Ibid.
32. Ibid., 24.

Holmer notes, "it is not about God at all but is only a history of someone's thoughts."[33]

This notion that theology is not simply "about" God or religious concerns but both reflects on the first-order language of faith and becomes part of this language is a point we noted earlier in our discussion of Holmer's reflections on Kierkegaard's writing. In Holmer's perspective on the logic of religious faith, knowledge "of" supersedes knowledge "about." It is in this sense that theology as grammar is not simply an articulation of the rules governing the proper use of language but is directed instead toward the actual grammatical speaking of this language. Indeed, according to Holmer, just as in learning grammar "speaking grammatically" is the real sign of understanding the grammar, "the grammar that is theology requires, objectively and necessarily, love and fear as the content of a person's Godliness. And the very knowledge that began in the "about" mood now becomes transformed into a 'how,' another mood altogether."[34]

As we have seen, it is this project of personal appropriation, language used in the "of" mood rather than the "about" mood that, in Holmer's view, is the necessary direction of theological reflection and teaching as well: "The whole business of using theology as grammar requires also that we refer our nation, our world, our selves and our future to God."[35] This is part of the "imaginative" project of theological interpretation and why, in addition to syllogisms and formal argumentation, theology employs the literary means of metaphors, parables, stories, informal conversation, everyday speech and allegory. The use of metaphor and parable is not a decorative addition to the prosaic factual content of theology but the necessary means by which theology properly becomes personally compelling and persuasive. This imaginative project of theology is not optional, but rather, as Holmer puts it, "the outworking of the language *about* faith when it becomes the language *of* faith."[36]

The centrality of the imagination to the work of theology has to do with its role in moving one to conceive the world and oneself in relation to God and therein, with becoming something new: namely, becoming a "child of God." Because such a perspective of life in relation to God is neither natural nor necessary, "imagination is the broker between what is

33. Ibid., 25.
34. Ibid.
35. Ibid., 26
36. Ibid., 27.

learned and what is, in consequence, possible."[37] Where theology may begin with content about the nature of God or the world as creation, it moves in the direction of helping us to conceive of ourselves as children of God and see the world as God's own. As Holmer writes: "The whole thrust of theology has to be in the direction not of finding something out—for that is only at the beginning—but rather of becoming something more worthy and justified."[38]

In conceiving of the task of theology in this manner Holmer is not saying that theology is a more meaningful kind of prose than everyday speech or the words of the Bible. He writes:

> It is a mistake to say that we have the Bible, on the one hand, and then its meaning stated in another tissue of prose altogether. The entire picture is wrong; and every pastor and theologian must resist that plain and insistent request for a statement of the meaning. Just as the meaning of a piece of logic is not another piece of prose about logic but the achievement of logical acuity and accuracy of thought and inference, so the meaning of Jesus' life and death is not a theory of the atonement or an elaborate Christology.[39]

Rather than viewing theology as that form of prose which "states the meaning" of the Bible or the historic creeds, the role of theology in Holmer's view is, again, more properly thought of in pedagogical terms. That is to say, the work of theology is not somehow to state what the primary sources of religious teaching fail to state plainly, but "as an active pedagogy," but rather to help place the listener into a new role, where "his self-evaluation, his subjectivity, his aims, wishes home and desires," are altered in such a way that the teachings "will spring to life for him."[40]

In Holmer's view, it is precisely this pedagogical role that prevents theology from degenerating into mere ideology. For whereas an ideology requires an allegiance to its own particular articulation, theology seeks instead to become transparent in such a way that we do not focus on it but "see everything else" in light of it. To see ourselves in light of God, to experience our need of hope and healing, to seek guidance in the midst of our lostness, all these become the province of a genuine theology concerned not with knowledge "about" God, but rather knowledge "of" God.

37. Ibid., 28.
38. Ibid.
39. Ibid.
40. Ibid., 29.

Despite its sometimes technical and seemingly esoteric character it is essential for Holmer that theology not be divorced from what he terms "the plain elements and words that fashion the Christian faith." If theology may in some ways be akin to theory, it nonetheless has specific and quite practical purposes. As Holmer understands it, theology is not an optional activity within the life of faith; rather, as he puts it, "it is the minimum and necessary awareness of God, by which counseling, Near Eastern archeology, soul-care, geriatric services, and parish life get their correct evaluation and even their point."[41] In this sense, theology is always in service to the larger purpose of helping to move persons to the point of hearing the message of Scripture, of the historic creeds and practices of the church as a message directed to their own life in such a way that a personal and passionate response is elicited. Indeed, it is precisely because faith cannot be directly mediated—as Kierkegaard emphasized so strongly—that theology has a role at all. As Holmer writes: "The knowledge of God does not get moved from one mind to another in a direct and immediate way. What we can mediate from one mind to another is Luther's thoughts, and the church fathers, the words of the apostles, and the meditations of a systematic theologian. By themselves, these are not the matters called 'knowing God'; but they are like a grammar and like a means with which you, the reader, come to know God."[42]

It is in this sense that theology may be said to transmit not knowledge of God but "the thought and action within which knowing God becomes a possibility."[43] This is part of the grammar of the concept of God and of "knowing God." And, as we will discuss in greater detail, that possibility is realized, according to Holmer's rendition of the grammatical character of Christian theology, in showing that the kind of knowing that knowing God is, is akin to a person. Knowledge in this sense is not accomplished by a single discrete act or occasion but happens over time by learning about a variety of things—what a person has done, his or her likes and dislikes, wishes and hopes, motives and actions over time.[44] It is for this same reason, according to Holmer, that it is important to know others who know

---

41. Ibid., 31.

42. Ibid., 31–32.

43. Ibid., 32.

44. This perspective on the nature of knowing a person is in keeping with Hans Frei's notion of how identity description is given as part of an unfolding narrative; see Frei, *The Identity of Jesus Christ.*

God, the reason that Scripture, the traditions of theological writing and the like are essential to the grammar of Christian theology. For it is by means of these writings and such personal testimonies that "the reader has come to know God by knowing all sorts of other things first."[45]

The grammar of the concept of God and the character of knowing God that theology describes also reinforce for Holmer the critical function of theology in challenging the use of Christianity as a means of rationalizing and forwarding causes that are extraneous to the faith. When this occurs and Christianity is valued primarily for its social implications rather than its transcendent content, theology is in danger of becoming a kind of religious ideology. Again, for Holmer, theology as the grammar of faith has a continual polemical function, "one of the ways that Christians learn to be on guard."[46] Because the specific content of the Christian message has a crucified savior at the center of the story, by delineating what it means to know the God revealed in Christ, Christian theology serves to challenge, for example, the identification of the Christian life with surges of sentiment that might instead be used to serve the state, totalitarian institutions or even moral aims. As Holmer writes: "Theology is that knowledge that tells us, also, all kinds of polemical things. If only because one knows God and who He is, one knows a lot, too, that is not of God. Therefore theology is always polemically poised; and it, too, like God himself, has to wound before it heals."[47]

Theology as grammar then both teaches and critiques. These pedagogical and the polemical aspects of theology are, for Holmer, interconnected and equally important. And this for the reason that, for Holmer, it is not primarily the content of the Christian faith that must be recast, but rather, the recipient. In forwarding the grammar of the faith—in helping us to understand who God is and who we are, what it means to know God and what this knowledge may effect in a human life—theology is in service to the education of our emotions, the knowledge of our need, the discernment of our situation, and the awakening of our hearts. In both these ways—by moving one to the point of personal appropriation and by articulating

45. Holmer, *Grammar of Faith*, 32. Holmer does not cite any specific passages from Wittgenstein, but his presentation here reflects Wittgenstein's notion of describing the grammar and logic of language specific language uses, in this case, "knowing a person" and "knowing God."

46. Ibid., 33.

47. Ibid.

criteria of critical judgment—theology becomes "the way by which know-ing God converts to serving him."[48]

We now turn to a more detailed examination of Holmer's critique of the contemporary theological scene and the constructive pedagogy he proposes in the subsequent chapters of *The Grammar of Faith*.

4. Theology and Belief

Following the lead of both Kierkegaard and Wittgenstein, the whole of Holmer's critique may be characterized as a polemic against the metaphysical presuppositions underlying much contemporary theology. In particular, Holmer castigates the pretension that the role of theology is to state "the understanding" somehow underlying or hidden within a more primitive language of faith. Holmer offers the example of a student of aesthetics telling an artist that the artist must first understand the principles of aesthetics before proceeding with his art as a situation akin to what often takes place in the realm of theology. While it is the very nature of religion and the re-ligious life to invite continual reflection, theology errs when it presumes to present "the understanding" or "the meaning" of religious faith by abstract-ing from the ordinary language and practices of the life of faith. According to Holmer, "there is something terribly wrong with thinking that every lin-guistic assertion needs explaining and unpacking, as if it were incomplete and partial until placed in a mutually enriching and artificial context of theological or metaphysical scheme."[49]

It is this assumption that "meaning" is elucidated by removing a lan-guage use from the ordinary context and practices with which it is nor-mally associated that is so troubling to Holmer. And he is direct in his view that this procedure is simply wrongheaded: "But to assume that there is 'an understanding' or 'several understandings' still waiting to be expressed, lying, as it were, in front of the text (like Plato's ideas in that famous story of the cave), still to be apprehended by great efforts—this surely is a mistake."[50]

In Holmer's view, rather than seeing contemporary critiques that biblical language and ancient theological formulations lack meaning for moderns as evidence of the limitations of metaphysical conceptualities, theologians continue to think that what they need is another conceptual

48. Ibid., 34.
49. Ibid., 43.
50. Ibid., 47.

system. As Holmer notes: "The trouble has been that, once bereft of one system of artifices of thought, we have been led to think that we cannot do or think anything sensible unless we have another."[51] The assumption underlying this perennial move in theology is that there are different levels of meaning and that the "meanings" theology presents are somehow clearer, more distinct and refined than the language of Scripture. Indeed, in this view, the words of Scripture are assumed to be a kind of temporary media of expression that by being translated into a more abstract and systematic conceptuality are made more accessible and enduring.

In contrast to this, what Holmer proposes is a more circumscribed role for theology. In relation to Scripture, for example, the task of theology is to help people understand "but not always by substituting general views, super-naturalistic, scholastic, ontological or secular for the specific passages, but rather by using every means . . . to get persons familiar and intimate with what the text requires."[52] Or again, rather than abstracting from the ordinary language and practices of the life of faith in an effort to present "the meaning" underlying them, the purpose of theology is "not to be God's revelation" but "to root believers in the Christian life."[53]

In all of this, as we have seen earlier in our examination of his reading of Kierkegaard and Wittgenstein, and again, in the beginning chapters of *The Grammar of Faith*, Holmer is directing attention to the "form of life" and the "how" of faith in addition to its content, arguing "the theologian has to be concerned with 'how,' for it is in the 'how' along with the 'what' that Christian concerns are enjoined."[54] We should make clear, however, that this concern on Holmer's part is a "logical" one relating to the logic and grammar of Christian beliefs. That is, the mode of appropriating Christian teachings forms the context for what it means to "understand" these teachings and is an essential component of the meaning and content of belief.

In reference to belief in God, for example, Holmer observes that "much of the Christian's confidence that there is a God who cares and loves comes, not from metaphysics, but from such odd things as the sense of guilt and the personal vicissitudes that guilt involves."[55] While Holmer concedes that it might be possible to separate out the concept of God from its place

51. Ibid.
52. Ibid., 49.
53. Ibid., 50.
54. Ibid., 51.
55. Ibid.

within a Christian outlook, the question of the Christian meaning of this concept can only be understood in reference to "what the word *God* did for people when they believed, prayed, worshipped, and perhaps tried to love him with all their heart, soul, mind and strength."[56] In a similar way, the work of the theologian in trying to make the Christian concept of God meaningful to others can only be accomplished, not by abstracting it from the context of Christian practices, but precisely by attending to them and thereby showing how this concept works from within this perspective.

Just as Holmer is strongly critical of the assumption that religious language requires translation into another form of philosophical or metaphysical discourse in order to ascertain its meaning, he is similarly critical of attempts to render the faith or religious language in the parlance of the natural sciences. In Holmer's polemic, such supposedly "objective" study of religion is often substituted for authentic theology with the promises that it will bring greater understanding and ensure a place for theology within the larger scholarly/scientific community. But Holmer argues that such an approach is problematic because scientific language and method are inappropriate to both the subject matter and the purpose of theology

The disinterested and neutral character of scientific language is the basis for its guarantees of communicability and universality and the move towards seeking a more objective, seemingly ordered study and language is understandable. Indeed, we must note that Holmer recognizes the adequacy and appropriateness of scientific study and language for certain components within the larger theological enterprise—a realm of religious studies, for example. It is not that there is no place for the scientific study of religious materials, but that such "objective" study of religion in neither the same as, nor required as a foundation for, theology as the grammar of faith.

Although religious language is not merely idiosyncratic or personally expressive, the internal ordering and grammar of its personal and confessional language stands in contrast to the dispassionate character of scientific language and study. The difference between these forms of discourse and their accompanying concerns and purposes is simply that—a difference: "The logic of the discourse of science is not the same as the logic of religion."[57] Because the purpose of theological reflection is to help convey the distinctive, personally-involving character of religious language, the detached orientation of the natural sciences is ill-suited to this subject matter.

56. Ibid., 52.
57. Ibid., 68.

"In this regard," writes Holmer, "it is appropriate to say that there can be no generic theory of meaning by which we say that scientific language is more meaningful than religious language or that . . . the language about religion is more meaningful than the theological kind we have just discussed."[58]

One place where this difference becomes apparent is in attending to the concept of "explanation" operative in these two realms. As Holmer notes, there are many kinds of explanation, each has its own context, and its own function, relative to a specific need:

> For a scientific explanation discloses the constituent circumstances of an event or a phenomenon and then the universal relations or laws by which these circumstances come to be as they are. A religious explanation is quite different in intent. Here a person seeks a justification for one's life in which the passion that is needful will find its correlatives in everything objective. The religious explanation is a direct use of pathos and does not resolve a dispassionate query or interest. Here a person seeks to know oneself and to explain everything relative to faith and to his or her God. So one can say that a religious explanation is a kind of achievement and hence a heightened instance of the religious life.[59]

Holmer goes on to observe that just as there is no necessary correlation between religious language and the scientific discourse about religion, there is no qualitative improvement in the language of religion because of a greater quantity of scientific scholarship about religious matters. The same may be said in reference to the relationship between scientific study and moral language. Here, again, a greater quantity of learning about ethical theory, for example, never necessitates the development of a moral consciousness. Holmer goes so far as to say that the languages of science and religious faith are not so much "different languages expressive of the same reality," whereby one might choose one over the other, but rather, in light of their differing categories and purposes, simply "incommensurable" with one another. This "incommensurability" means that the languages can neither confirm, contradict, nor replace one another.[60] Where they may come in conflict is if the language of cognition, i.e., the language of science, moves beyond its particular and limited cognitive interest to become a dominant

58. Ibid.

59. Ibid., 69.

60. This question of the "incommensurability" versus the incompatibility of scientific and religious explanation and its connection to the criticism that Holmer's position here is fideistic and relativistic will be addressed in more detail in the next chapter.

and exclusive enthusiasm which displaces religious and moral concern. On the other hand, according to Holmer, the claims about inspiration, infallibility, inerrancy and the like, on the part of some religious believers evince a denial of the objective uncertainties that are a necessary part of ethical pathos and religious faith.

5. The Quest for Foundations

A significant feature of what the cognitive prejudice for scientific methodology and language over the language of faith within the scholarly theological community both presupposes and perpetuates is the "search for foundations" in theology. In Holmer's view, however, this quest for foundations is mistaken. The assumption at work is the quite understandable and often earnest one that religion, like a building, must have a solid foundation, a ground, on which it is based. Holmer acknowledges the straightforward assumption, for example, that a report must have some foundation in fact if it is not to be judged as being "baseless." In a sense similar to buildings requiring physical foundations, we also speak of institutions being "founded" on an underlying principle or charter. Arguing by analogy then, we go on to think of groups of ideas or systems of thought as also requiring such foundations. The problem, according to Holmer, is that we are "led by a metaphor to the notion that groups of ideas must also have 'foundations' which are the ground, the basis, the support and the underlying base."[61]

Holmer questions this quite commonplace assumption by noting that the analogy, while understandable, is not so obvious as it may first appear:

> Of course, likening beliefs, not least religious beliefs (say the Apostles' Creed, the Thirty-nine Articles, or the Westminster Confession), to a building, as if both needed "foundations," is a little peculiar, after all. For beliefs, even those noted, must be believed, cared about, and put to all kinds of purposes. . . .The practice of comparing buildings (with foundations) and edifices of thought (again with foundations) supposes that those beliefs are separable from "saying," "telling," "singing," "saying," etc.[62]

As Holmer goes on to challenge the applicability of the analogy of buildings to beliefs he notes that "we do have buildings without the builders, but

61. Ibid., 82.
62. Ibid., 84.

there is an odd sense in which we do not have beliefs without believers. Without the latter, the beliefs are really nothing at all."[63] To abstract a belief from the activities with which it is associated and the purposes to which it is put, may be in keeping with the metaphor of buildings and foundations, but it misrepresents the actual character of beliefs.

The critique of the present state of religious belief and language by much contemporary theology is, of course, that these, too, are in need of foundations and the ones most often suggested are "metaphysical" foundations. Holmer examines and critiques two such proposed "metaphysical foundations," namely, Martin Heidegger's ontology and what he terms "the search for facts."

Foundation in Being

It is clear from the very start of his examination that Holmer has little sympathy for either the search for foundations or Heidegger's ontology in particular, and the polemical character of his presentation throughout is noteworthy.[64] While we will not examine all the details of his argumentation, Holmer offers what amounts to a Wittgensteinian or "ordinary language" analysis of the basic metaphysical orientation of ontology.

Holmer begins by noting the general assumption at work in Heidegger's (and by implication, Paul Tillich's) ontology; namely, that words and names for things that exist—like the things themselves—have something akin to an "essence" in common. This common essence, according to Heidegger, is "the very general and indispensable concept of 'being.'"[65] Somewhat tongue-in-cheek, Holmer adds: "Apparently this is what many people think a real foundation is, for it is as if one cannot get anything more basic, more fundamental, nearer the bottom of anything and everything."[66]

63. Ibid.

64. It would appear that it is the ontology of the Heidegger in *Being and Time* that is the primary subject of Holmer's critique as then represented by New Testament theologian Rudolph Bultmann and systematic theologian Paul Tillich, although he later specifically names Karl Rahner as one "infatuated" with the possibility that the concept of "being" will restore vitality to theology (ibid., 93). The essay "About Linguisticality and Being Able to Talk" included in *Thinking the Faith With Passion* also provides evidence that Holmer was familiar with—and critical of—the later writings of Heidegger.

65. Quote attributed to Martin Heidegger without citation, in Holmer, *Grammar of Faith*, 86.

66. Holmer, *Grammar of Faith*, 91.

Holmer notes that in common parlance we often refer to the various things that exist by using, for example, the terms "this" or "that" as in "this" x or "that" y. Heidegger's ontological philosophy goes on to suggest that ideas or concepts which may be distinguished in this same way nonetheless share something in common because they both "are." Whereas in the case of general concepts traditionally termed "universals," the general concepts are seen as correlatives to individual concepts, e.g., "mankind" and "men," in the case of "being" everything that is is conceived as somehow sharing in this fundamental essence. Holmer does not bother to go into the details of Heidegger's presentation because what is at issue for him is the very first move of such an ontology wherein it is assumed that the predicate of "existing" or "having being" somehow counts as a significant link between things or the words used to refer to them. He writes: "My point here is not to discuss these [particulars of the argument]; for the validity of such arguments, transcendental or not, does not depend upon what is said after one lumps all 'existents' together, but on the propriety, indeed, of doing this kind of lumping at all."[67]

Again, Holmer's interest is not so much in critiquing the specific argumentation of Heidegger's or Tillich's ontology as to question the initial assumption which induces one to think that the concept of "being" is somehow implied or contained within our use of concepts. In this view, concepts are seen to be linked together in a kind of system or whole where "being" serves as the fundamental concept and ground of all else. But as Holmer argues: "There is a great difference between noting that concepts are rule-like, established ways of referring, for example, and hence dependent upon contexts, societies, ways of living, thinking, and explaining, and saying that all concepts are in a system. To deny the latter is not to deny the former."[68]

Together with those assumptions we have already noted, the particular philosophical issue at stake here—from a linguistic analysis perspective—is that of the grammar of the terms "reference" and "referring." Holmer writes:

> The reason for stating all of this is to show that theologians who began to cast about for something upon which they could base the theological teachings, tie them all down, show how they start perhaps and how they all mean (for all of these different things get lumped together in the search for "foundations") are frequently led to "being" and the concept of "being." Ontology seems to be

67. Ibid., 88.
68. Ibid., 90.

a general way to show that what the theologian is talking about really does, after all, refer to something.[69]

Where, on the one hand, ontology serves a supposed explanatory function by grouping together these various—and properly, distinct—issues of the origins, connections and meaning of beliefs, the notion that ontology and its reference to "being" provides the reference and therefore the meaning of religious language calls forth Holmer's strongest polemic:

> When the questioner, the doubter of divinity, who thinks it is all words, wants to know what it is all about and asks: 'Is there anything to it?'; the answer is: 'Of course. It has its foundation in being.' If this does not work, one can try the other side of the avenue: 'Every one of your concepts already refers to being and you do not know it. Theology only needs to make the ontological reference clear in all of our language in order to find its place. Theology is the science of meaning, too.' Or to carry the matter to ludicrous extremes, it is proposed that ordinary religious language is symbolical and at least once removed, whereas theology of this being-variety is conceptual, explanatory, technical, and clearer (albeit less religiously powerful and emotive).[70]

On the one hand, Holmer notes the absurdity of requiring an ontological statement to demonstrate that Christian teachings are referential and therefore have meaning:

> Usually we do not have to say two things—first, "I am leaving for Paris tomorrow," and second, "I refer to so and so" or "the whole sentence is meant to be taken thus and so." Is the language of the church different? Most of the time, language that has any genuineness to it at all does not refer all by itself anyway, nor does it have an accompanying ontological commentary which tells us how to take it. People (not words or concepts) who speak and write refer to all kinds of things, including God, and when we understand them we occupy ourselves appropriately.[71]

As we have noted elsewhere, the question of "reference" is one that must be addressed in light of the activities and purposes of the person doing the referring. This is Holmer's point when he says that it is not words or concepts but people who refer. Indeed, he questions the very premise that religious

69. Ibid., 91
70. Ibid.
71. Ibid., 91–92.

language has somehow lost its referential function and use. For when language is used referringly, in Holmer's terms, "the reference is not secured by the language nor by another ratifying 'ontological' scheme; rather the speaker or the writer does the referring. . . . Reference is not a trick, a subtle bit of learning, or even a matter of insight."[72] The fact of the matter is that people "refer" all the time and in a myriad of different ways, using words, gestures, and a variety of formal and informal techniques; reference is not secured by a recourse to another conceptual system. For this reason, Holmer is sharply critical of the pretense of theologies that look to ontology to provide a foundation, noting that "the notion that a concept, especially one like that of 'being,' will restore vitality to a kind of general theology seems to me downright ludicrous."[73]

Foundation in Fact

A second effort to "ground" theological and religious language is what Holmer terms, "the search for the facts." Although we have previously noted some of the permutations of this move in our examinations of Holmer's earlier discussion of the relation of scientific language to religious language and in his challenge to the primacy of historical interpretation, his analysis here is noteworthy for his extended reflection on the concept of "fact."

As in the case of the search for foundations, Holmer notes that it is quite understandable that the issue of the factual content of religious faith gets raised. Questions such as "Was there a Jesus or not?" or "Did God make the world or didn't he?" and others are commonplace and unexceptional. In the same manner, the perceived need and desire to ground the faith in "facts" is simply another version of the search for foundations itself: "One can understand . . . how the question becomes fundamental. For if there is nothing 'factual,' then our habits easily lead us to say there are only illusions, opinions, interpretations, theories, speculations, generalizations, fancies, fictions, art, etc."[74] Therefore, issues of fact—was there a Jesus, are the ten commandments a divine gift or human invention, and a host of others—are in part invited by the very nature of the Scriptural witness. However, there is an additional concern in the search for "the facts"—namely, it

72. Ibid., 92.
73. Ibid., 93.
74. Ibid., 96.

is assumed that questions of fact must be raised and answered before one commits oneself to a religious faith.

Although the impetus to seek foundations, and in particular, to obtain one grounded in "the facts" may be both understood and critiqued in the above manner, the real issue at stake is the concept of "fact" itself. For as Holmer notes, and as we have touched on earlier, there are many sorts of "facts." On the one hand, there are various modes of research that have as their avowed goal and aim examination of "the facts." Literary and historical investigations are, of course, two of the favored approaches when dealing with Scripture or the history of the Christian faith and its teachings. Whether or not such approaches are sufficient for the task of understanding religious belief is one issue; whether they may serve in some way to "ground" the faith is another. To suggest reservations in regard to the former proposal, as we have already noted, does not exhaust the reasons for challenging the possibility of the latter. As Holmer observes: "There are all kinds of facts and all kinds of concepts of fact. But the difficulty here is that what is legitimate—namely a resolute search for this or that—lends its genuineness to the creation of another concept, a master concept of 'fact *qua* fact.'"[75] That is, it is not merely the search for "facts" appropriate to different research methodologies that is at stake—as insufficient as any one of these methodologies may be—but rather, the attempt to locate some kind of "ultimate" or "undeniable" fact that can, therein, serve as a foundation upon which one could then base a theology. The notion of fact as in "foundation in fact . . ." when used in theological contexts is, as Holmer notes, "at best, a borrowed usage from historical and scientific contexts, and, at worst, an inflated and ill-begotten posit, trading on some intellectual conventions but quite without substance."[76] It is this "inflated, ill-begotten" concept that is at work in the search for the "factual foundations" of theology: "For the theological quest for the fact is richly invested with a meaning-content like this—that there must be some neutral and nontheological facts, which because they are facts, are also indisputable, definitive, religiously neutral, unanalyzable, and the warrant for, the cause of, as well as the correlative to the theological statements."[77] What Holmer perceives at the heart of the search for theological foundations is this search for "non-theological" facts. And it is here that we come face to face with the real issue at stake.

75. Ibid., 99.
76. Ibid., 98.
77. Ibid.

For if, as we have noted, there is no such thing as a context-free fact, it is, in Holmer's analytical assessment, this very general and mistaken concept of fact that misleads us into thinking that there is such a thing, such a "fact," awaiting our discovery. Summarizing the various attempts to "found" the faith in a quest for the "historical Jesus," Holmer writes: "Despite valiant attempts to find the foundation of theology in facts about Jesus, nothing very conclusive ever appears to have been achieved. The pages of recent literature are strewn indeed with all kinds of researches, very refined and very detailed, but nothing that discloses a fact which could serve as a foundation, a guaranteed and indubitable starting point, something certain, simple, and also nontheological."[78]

The problematic of the search for foundations has not, however, been resolved in light of these failures. Holmer sees continuing attempts for historical and factual foundations at work in the proposals for a new and revised concept of fact defined in reference to a larger conceptual system.[79] In light of the perennial, and apparently irrepressible, character of this search for foundations, Holmer again turns to the concept of fact, observing that it "is not singular at all." He continues:

> There are indeed careful uses of "fact" in historical disciplines, just as there are in the natural sciences. At one time, people assumed that theological statements had their foundation in historical facts. The quest became very earnest, but it turns out that historical facts are just historical, and little else. They resolve historical doubts and play their roles primarily in an historian's context. So, too, with the scientific facts, be what they may. The hard lesson to learn is that there is no transposition from one to the other. Theological statements, finally, if reducible at all, are reducible only to theological facts.[80]

Holmer goes on to articulate his argument by noting what he views as neither a theory nor a proposal, but rather, simply a descriptive rendering of the concept: "for the meaning of 'fact,' the very concept, is not single at all—it varies with the intellectual context such that there is no one concept of fact; rather, there are many of them, and they do not overlap very

78. Ibid., 100.

79. Holmer cites Heinrich Ott and what was termed the "new quest" for the historical Jesus as such attempts, along with redefinitions of the concept of history in Collingwood, H. R. Niebuhr, and F. R. Tennant, among others.

80. Holmer, *Grammar of Faith*, 101–2.

significantly."[81] In order to understand the meaning of the term "fact" one must pay attention to the uses it is put to—to what it does—in the particular language domain in which it is used. Given the context-dependent character of the concept, it is simply mistaken to assume one common or core meaning in all instances where the word "fact" is used. As Wittgenstein noted, we are under the influence of a misleading picture when we assume that there are indisputable and elemental states of affairs that can be discovered independent of our particular domains of research and knowledge. And this mistaken picture influences even our search for God. It is not appropriate, in Holmer's view, to posit the picture of a "God's-eye" perspective, the context of a "God who knows everything," one for whom "states of affairs and facts correspond perfectly," for such a notion "is neither a religious concept of God nor a meaningful one; and certainly it does little for the concept of fact. Anyway, it is very questionable whether most people need to know what God knows in order to become devout."[82]

Of course, the argument may be made that the hypothetical possibility of such a context-free or universal perspective serves as the ideal or goal of human knowledge and judgments of truth and falsity; but as we have seen, and will explore further in our final chapter, Holmer denies the meaningfulness of such a projection of the concept of fact. Rather, "'fact' always marks a distinction between what is *not* disputed 'now,' 'here,' 'in this context,' 'under these circumstances,' 'presently,' and what *is* so disputed"; even within the realm of a particular discourse the concept of "fact" is not unequivocal for "there is no big fact, final fact, discoverable by . . . any kind of research into facts."[83] As he goes on to write: "Usually what we call a fact is what we can reason from, what we can take for granted, what is agreed upon, and what (in this context, place, and for given purposes) we do not need to quarrel about and perhaps cannot. In this limited sense there are facts; but these are disputable the moment we learn how to raise questions that are relevant, and sometimes from very different contexts."[84]

By incorporating the perspectives of the language analysis of Wittgenstein, J. L. Austin, and other "ordinary language" philosophers, Holmer is challenging a fundamental presupposition at work in our use of general concepts showing that their definitions are never applicable in a single or

---

81. Ibid., 102.
82. Ibid., 103.
83. Ibid., 104.
84. Ibid., 105.

univocal manner. In this same way he is suggesting the limits of human knowledge and the absence of both the need for, and the possibility of, a single "foundation":

> It is simply a mistake to assume that empirical research and historical study will some day reveal "the fact," in virtue of which the foundation for theology will be laid once and for all. The fault is again not in the researches, in methods, in subject matter, or in skills or lack thereof; it is, rather, in the very concept of fact, the inflated and fantastic concept, that promises to fit every kind of inquiry and ground the most strenuous and different endeavors, not least morals and religion.[85]

The search for a foundation, mistaken though it may be in the forms critiqued by Holmer, is not wholly dismissed. For there are indeed foundations, according to Holmer, conceptual, factual and other. But it is clear for Holmer that in the two major options pursued in order to establish a foundation for theological reflection, theologians have been misled by the words "being" and "fact." But perhaps there is an appropriate use—or better, "uses"—of the concept of "fact" in reference to religious language; indeed, as Holmer notes, there are certain "facts" which are important for the Christian faith:

> . . . Christian people have for a couple of thousand years attached great significance to the fact of *Consumatum est*. Something was settled and is therefore ready; some things have been done; sin and death are vanquished; God is in Christ, and Christ has been born, has lived, has died, and been raised from the dead. In a certain way of speaking, these together make the fact, the foundation, of at least Christian theology.[86]

Even saying this, however, the caveat must be added that historical facts are not the foundation for theological assertions, nor are they sufficient to establish anything beyond the historical fact of Jesus' existence. But those other "facts" to which Christians refer and refer themselves—that God was in Christ, that sin and death have been overcome—are neither given a foundation in historical fact nor, it will be argued, require one. Rather, they suggest the kind of "facts" which are the province of religious interest and its concomitant ways of knowing. To address these we now turn to Holmer's final chapters in *The Grammar of Faith*.

85. Ibid., 106.
86. Ibid., 109.

6. Concepts and Capacities

Given his critique of much of the academic and scholarly reflection about religion, Holmer might easily be seen as an anti-intellectualist and his focus on the practices and behavioral components of religious faith may suggest he is a proponent of a kind of experiential or even pietistic religion. While Holmer agrees with John Wesley's remark that faith is not a matter of "cold, rational assent," and, with Wesley, speaks of faith as a "disposition of the heart," it would be wrong to type him as an advocate of the primacy of personal experience over reflection. Although Holmer is quite sympathetic to those who emphasize "experience" as a response to the problematic posed by the plethora of contemporary theologies, he is critical of the move that would substitute either religious feeling and enthusiasm or ethics for theological reflection. As we have seen, Holmer views "experience" as an essential component of religious faith but always as linked with Christian teaching and theology. According to Holmer, "the Christian's life is a living synthesis of will, thought, and pathos, all three."[87] Holmer recognizes that the traditional emphasis on doctrines and teachings, and, therefore, on the cognitive dimension of religious faith has often been "at the expense of the volitional, the ethical and the affectional," and that, in response, there has been a counter movement stressing the latter. But because the teachings of the faith are essential and formative for the personal language of faith and because this language is not merely expressive, Holmer argues for a theological perspective that involves both rigorous conceptual reflection and attention to the pathos and subjectivity that are essential to the lived experience of religious faith. The connection of these elements or concerns is shown by his examination of the nature of "concepts" and his description analysis of the grammar of some specific Christian concepts.

Holmer notes early on a working definition—or, more accurately, a formal description—of concepts as "a meaning-complex." What he means in a very general sense is that a concept is not simply a word or name for which a definition can be offered or reference pointed to, but rather a complex of meaning by means of which we refer and make assertions: "So concepts like 'man,' 'animal,' and 'thing,' as well as 'God,' 'grace,' . . . are minimally the means by which we refer. When we assert something about something . . . then we must use concepts. Concepts empower our asserting, for they give us something to talk about."[88]

87. Ibid., 137.
88. Ibid., 139.

In terming a concept a "meaning complex" Holmer is not trading on the distinction we often make between words and meaning—as though words are the physical marks and meanings something spiritual or mental expressed by the words—but instead, on the difference between words as physical marks or noises and the uses to which they are put. As Holmer presents it, the criterion for understanding a concept is not "being able to define it but to be able to do the proper things with it."[89] Concepts are used, in this sense, to judge, evaluate, describe, consider, and the like, and to understand a concept as a meaning complex is to be able to use it in such ways.

As Holmer tries to make clear, he is not proposing a "mentalist picture" of words as spiritual entities or "meanings" which exist prior to the use of a word or phrase. Rather, according to his description, "They [concepts] are more like personal powers, like potencies, like skills and abilities . . ."[90] Rather than being learned by means of a definition, it is, as we have noted, by learning what it is that they enable one to do with them—referring, describing, judging—that one can be said to "have" a concept. In this sense, concepts may be compared to tools or instruments: as one learns how to use them, a kind of skill or ability is realized that allows one to accomplish a variety of tasks. It is these competencies and abilities, "the enabling for a variety of tasks, that is the complex we call a concept."[91]

The use of concepts is not limited to speaking or writing but extends to non-linguistic practices as well. As Holmer writes, "We are indebted to concepts for changed dispositions, for creating and sustaining emotions, for enlarging sympathy, for stimulating passion, and even for creating the virtues."[92] Citing Wittgenstein's maxim, "How words are understood is not told by words alone," Holmer notes that a theological concept like "holiness" has "the power of converting a person from unholiness to holiness," adding that if the concept does not begin to do this, "we have good reason for saying that one has misunderstood it."[93] This non-linguistic component is especially important in the use of concepts that theology employs, reminding its practitioners that the meaning of religious concepts is not demonstrated in discourse alone but by the new quality and form of life they engender:

89. Ibid., 140.

90. Ibid.

91. Ibid., 142.

92. Ibid., 143.

93. Ibid., 143–44. The quote from Ludwig Wittgenstein is found in *Zettel*, No. 144.

> Thus it is important to remember that what we are saying about concepts does not suggest that concepts are initially spiritual and mental and that they subsequently get translated into either speech or deeds. The linguistic employment is not a translation at all. For concepts are not present to the mind in a nonlinguistic way first and then only exemplified and deployed in verbal fashion afterwards. Here the orientation is wrong. The point is, rather, that concepts have as part of their meaning, part of the complex, this power to be extended in speech.[94]

The implications of this perspective for the practice and teaching of theology, in keeping with the ongoing theme of *The Grammar of Faith*, are of primary concern to Holmer. On the one hand, according to Holmer, one of the primary tasks of theology is "the description and study of religious concepts." As religious concepts have become entangled with systems of other concepts, the theologian's task—à la Wittgenstein—is the "disentangling" of these concepts. But paralleling the distinction already noted at length that Holmer draws between a theology in the "about" mood and religious language in the "of" mood, he observes: "It is one thing to use the concepts and quite another thing to teach theology in such a way that the upshot is the actual employment of these concepts by the pupil."[95] Where one consequence of such theological reflection and teaching might be that some pupils learn to do theology, the more significant use of these concepts is to aid in the formation of a religious life. Holmer seems to leave open whether teachers of theology are obliged to attempt the latter, but he does suggest that religious teachers "might want to insist that religion itself is a kind of education, quite different from what one would otherwise acquire."[96] As "those ruled functions in our lives that we can characterize and give names to," the use of concepts extends far beyond just talking about the concepts themselves, to include creating new motivations and a new conception of one's life. In light of this, the purpose—if not the practice—of theological discourse properly incorporates these larger concerns: "Thus we can say about the concepts proposed by the religious literature that they are discoursed about at length in theological treatises, that hopefully they permit their users to talk and think about God and the world, but also that they can be employed to refashion one's life and even to remake

94. Ibid., 144.
95. Ibid.
96. Ibid., 145.

the world."[97] The purpose of religious teaching is, in the end, not merely to discuss concepts but to commission disciples. "Therefore," according to Holmer, "to understand theology and to evince a command of its concepts is to be spurred, to be humiliated, to be stirred to contrition, to be prepared for joy."[98]

Holmer goes on to note what he sees to be some distinctive features of Christian concepts. On the one hand, Holmer notes that some concepts grow up within the context of a specialized field or discipline. Within the realm of theological studies itself there are such specialized fields and accompanying technical concepts. In addition, there are those more general concepts—e.g., "object," "event," "thing"—which seem to have a kind of enduring quality or even non-historical character, such that they continue in both vernacular and specialized discourse. By noting this, Holmer challenges what he sees as a prevailing notion that all concepts are in the process of change, waxing and waning over time. As an example of such a "non-historical concept," Holmer cites the example of the concept "I." According to Holmer, "I" was never a technical or specialized concept, but is straightforwardly linked to what might be termed a general fact—that there are such things as persons and persons talk about themselves—and functions without the need of either overt training or justification. It is to this "class" of concepts that Holmer believes aesthetic, moral and religious concepts belong, and that such concepts have a "correspondence" with what he calls "general facts."

As an example of the correspondence of a religious concept with such a "general fact" Holmer suggests that the concept of "faith" is "not an arbitrary invention," but instead has to do "with a range of uncertainties, on the one side, and the human need for resolving one's fate amid these uncertainties, on the other."[99] This notion of a concept being linked up with what appear to be the perennial concerns and preoccupation of human beings, originating apart from specialized interests, suggests at least an informal definition of what might constitute "the facts" to which certain religious concepts are used to refer. But more importantly, Holmer is arguing for seeing the connection between such a religious concept and the functions it performs and enables in a human life. In reference to the concept "God," Holmer argues that "it is not a wild fabrication . . . invented and then

97. Ibid.
98. Ibid., 146.
99. Ibid., 151.

imposed by fiat or custom on the unwilling" but instead has "an odd fitting-ness over the centuries" which is seen in how it functions in a human life: "For having the concept 'God' is also to have certain set of functions in one's life. If one knows how to use the word *God* in prayer and worship, then one has the concept. One can do all sorts of things with the concept 'God'—for example, one can explain, praise, and curse. One can even attain peace of mind and forgiveness of sin. The concept is crucial to a way of life and a view of life."[100] Holmer's argument here is that the concept of "God" has "a kind of location and place in our lives" that is more fundamental than overt definitions or specialized theological discourse, even suggesting the possibility that it "is often the genesis more than the result of our religious thinking."[101] Although Holmer does not pursue this last suggestion, his point is that, as a concept, the concept of God has connections both with some universal aspects of human life and, more specifically, with certain practices and activities that form a way of life. As he writes: "To believe in God is like finding a little hope when all is depressing around you; to trust in God is like taking heart when you seem to have no right to it. These are minimal surroundings for the concept 'God' that make it vital."[102]

This is not to say that all concepts can simply be grouped together, or that all uses of a concept are the same. Indeed, according to Holmer, there are some distinctive uses and particular capacities that are connected with the religious, and more specifically, the Christian use, of the concept of God. In the case of Christianity, it may be said that in order to live a Christian life one "has to acquire some things, among them emotions, vir-tues, and also those capacities we have called concepts," for "one needs to know how to love, to hope, and what to believe—all of these taken together begin to provide the conditions by which a person can forge his or her own life in a manner that is distinctively Christian."[103] And yet, according to Holmer, "Christianity does not always introduce the concept "God," but rather, "Christian teachings trade upon it, modifying by reference to the person of Jesus and extending it to all kind of additional circumstances."[104] Once again Holmer is emphasizing both the difference between, and the respective importance of, the language "of" faith and language "about" the

100. Ibid., 152.
101. Ibid.
102. Ibid., 153.
103. Ibid.
104. Ibid.

faith: "One need not also be able to talk about the concept or to define it in an ostensible manner. A successful use is a sufficient sign of mastery. There is a language of faith that is not only a sign of faith but also a part of the faith. To speak about that language of faith is an achievement of scholarship and one form of theologizing; but to speak so that those concepts authorize one's speech . . . [is] to use the concepts and not to talk about them."[105]

In the same way, the distinction between the content of Christian teachings and their appropriation—what Holmer terms, respectively, the "what" and the "how" of Christianity—is exemplified in the way that concepts as capacities form one's life. For, as Holmer contends, "there is a way to love, hope, care, respond, be joyful, and be sorrowful that is tied up very intimately with the 'what'":

> The "what" is ordinarily proposed in judgments about God and the world—what we have been calling theology. The "how" is, in part, a nonverbal way to employ the same components that make the judgments possible. This is not a matter of thoughts being expressed in action; rather, what authorizes, even requires, non-verbal behavior. Emotions, feelings, acts of mercy, confidence, hope for daily life—these and more are equally ingredient. The "how" can also be said to sometimes come before the "what"; and our reason for saying this is simply the Scripture itself, which shows how the theological teachings (and some parts thereof) on some occasions followed the acquisition of the "how."[106]

In Holmer's particular version of Kierkegaard's distinction between the "what" and the "how" of Christianity there is no hard and fast way of determining which comes first; rather, just as they are in the concepts themselves, "what" and "how" are woven together and intimately interrelated. In this same way, religious concepts work in such a way—as idea complexes and capacities—that attitudes, feelings, passions, and a host of other behavior patterns, are part of, and not simply the applications of, the force and meaning of these concepts.

7. Knowing God

One of the traditional responses to the question, "What is theology?" is to answer by means of analogy with the natural sciences. From this perspective,

105. Ibid., 154.
106. Ibid., 155.

theology is the rational knowledge of God, or, perhaps more accurately, the objective study of God, which offers such knowledge. It is Holmer's contention—as we have noted repeatedly—that this analogy with the natural sciences is both misleading and mistaken for theology. Although theology is clearly oriented towards the knowledge of God, it is, according to Holmer, another kind of knowledge than that offered by the natural sciences that it seeks. This "other kind of knowledge" is required both by the logic of the concept "God" (and other religious concepts) and the nature of theological reasoning.

Holmer challenges a dominant theme of the Western intellectual tradition, namely, the notion of a "singular and sovereign rationality" which is common to all pursuits of knowledge. This aspect of a common intellectual tradition tends to go unchallenged as applied to theology insofar as it is seen to be only the minimal, necessary, and formal requirement for giving shape and discipline to theological inquiry as well as any other. From within this orientation, Holmer observes, it is assumed that nothing "substantive is supposedly being proposed if one requires evidence, asks for justification, and seeks for answers."[107]

Holmer recognizes at the same time that there have been challenges to this tradition. Martin Luther, Søren Kierkegaard, and Karl Barth are noted as among those who have questioned the idea that there are single and unequivocal concepts of reason, logic, objectivity and criteria to which theological inquiry must conform. Although Holmer questions the characterization of Kierkegaard and Barth as proposing that all knowledge of God comes through special revelation alone, he agrees that they both in their own way forward a view of theology at odds with the notion that it is, or should be, a wholly objective and rational study seeking neutral knowledge of God.

To Kierkegaard, Luther, and Barth as the alleged representatives of an anti-rational, "subjectivistic" perspective, the name of Wittgenstein has been added in light of his remarks about the foundational character of "forms of life." As Holmer notes: "If forms of life are foundational, then it looks as though fideism is more crucial than theology."[108] And as we will discuss in the next chapter, Holmer himself has been characterized as a representative of what is termed the "Kierkegaardian-Wittgensteinian paradigm" or "Wittgensteinian fideism."[109] As Holmer observes, how-

107. Ibid., 182.

108. Ibid., 184.

109. The designation "Kierkegaardian-Wittgensteinian paradigm" is employed by

ever, it is only with a particular—and limited—notion of what constitutes "rationality" in mind that these characterizations are made: "So it is that followers of Wittgenstein and Wittgenstein himself are assumed to be of the mind that denies that there is a recognizable kind of knowledge of God and that therefore theology is not truly cognitive, objective and rational. Oddly enough, Barthians, Kierkegaardians, and Wittgensteinians together look like the opponents of cognitivity and rationality in religion, but only if a certain pattern of rationality is taken to be normative."[110]

Holmer is without doubt the representative of an alternative perspective or interweaving of perspectives influenced by Luther, Kierkegaard, Barth and Wittgenstein, among others, but whether it may be properly characterized as either a "paradigm" or as "fideistic" is questionable. What Holmer does straightforwardly challenge on the basis of his own analysis of theological and religious discourse is the notion that these activities are to be understood and evaluated in light of a direct analogy to the knowledge sought and secured by the physical and social sciences. Holmer states his position directly when he writes: "It is the thesis of these pages that when Christianity is made into something primarily theological and doctrinal, then the nature of the faith becomes malformed, as if it were chiefly an act of belief in the doctrine. Subsequently, every person would then be required to understand the theology, and the gist of being a Christian would be a matter of comprehension, just as one might say that being a geologist is a matter of ever deepening and broadening the intellectual grasp."[111]

According to Holmer, the work of theologians like Kierkegaard and Barth has served to raise doubts about some of the traditional conceptions of the methods and purpose of theological reflection and system-building. In addition, philosophers like Wittgenstein have forced us to see on grounds independent of theology or metaphysics the limits of reasoning in one realm after another and "how the harmony between thought and reality, between what is said and what is, is to be found in the rules and structures of the language itself."[112] It is for this reason that Holmer's own analysis focuses on

---

Cornel West in his Review of *The Grammar of Faith*, 284. D. Z. Phillips comments on these labels in his "Grammarians and Guardians," 25: "The academic practitioners can breathe a sigh of relief, a new label has been provided, and now *it* can be discussed. This would have undoubtedly been the fate of the Wittgensteinian-Kierkegaardian paradigm has not another label, Wittgensteinian fideism, beat it in consumer appeal."

110. Holmer, *Grammar of Faith*, 184.

111. Ibid., 185.

112. Ibid. In a footnote, Holmer notes Wittgenstein's observation in *Zettel*, 12: "Like

the issues of faith and Christian practice. As Wittgenstein has shown, (and in Holmer's view this is not a theory but a description), "there is no single and comprehensive logic, no univocal and necessary kind of reason, the same for all domains"; rather is it the case that human reasoning is "polymorphic, depending upon the interests and subject matter, and therefore the 'grammars,' the 'logics,' are various."[113] This critique, as we have demonstrated repeatedly, does not mean that there is no logic or grammar to the Christian faith or the language of faith but that it has its own particular logic. And this is why, in Holmer's view, theology is properly conceived of as the "grammar of faith," and "has a subservient but crucial role in producing the consciousness of God."[114] It is to this issue of "knowing God" and the role of theology in aiding its achievement that we now turn.

The Concept of Knowing

As we have noted in reference to other concepts like "fact," "knowing" is also, according to Holmer, always "context-determined." "Knowing," then, does not consist in any one thing and the concept of knowing "turns out not to be a standard state of mind, nor is it a mode of consciousness or a process."[115] As an example, Holmer contrasts knowing a person's name with knowing the person named: "In the first instance, I show my knowledge by a referring use of a word; in the second instance, I evince my knowledge of a person, even if I cannot remember his or her name, by citing characteristics, predicting responses, describing propensities, attributing motives, and noting all kinds of other intimate matters. I either know the name or I do not . . . but knowing a person calls for understanding, and that one has more likely in degree and never in a single context."[116] By noting these differences, and others, in the use of the concept "knowing," Holmer observes that the "highly generalized idea" that all knowledge is propositional does not begin to do justice to the various kinds of knowing: "To know a person,

---

everything metaphysical the harmony between thought and reality is to be found in the grammar of the language."

113. Ibid.

114. Ibid.

115. Ibid., 186.

116. Ibid., 187.

a name, or mathematics is not very significantly described as 'knowing,' or 'entertaining,' or 'believing' a proposition."[117]

Holmer looks at the case of what is involved when we speak of "knowing oneself": "The person who is importuned by follies and envy that can never be satisfied is justly said to be without self-knowledge. Here a lack of knowledge bespeaks lack of self-clarification and all kinds of resolutions of will and spirit."[118] Knowledge, in this case, has little to do with believing in propositions. As we have suggested, something similar is at work when we speak about the language of faith, for it, too, can be said to involve, both as a condition and as a result, a kind of self-knowledge.

Once again what Holmer is pointing out is that by attending to, by describing and comparing the various uses of a concept, one comes to see not one meaning in all contexts, but precisely the differences in meaning which are gathered around one term. In Wittgenstein's parlance, these meanings may share a "family resemblance"—in one context sharing some common features, in other contexts, other similarities; but, akin to the resemblances shared by members of a family, there is no one core or essence constituting the resemblance in all cases. Although the same term "know" is used in these different settings, it is attention to the context and use that is the means to understanding the particular nuances in the meaning of the term. It is this description of the context and uses which reveals the "grammar" of the concept within a particular language use or "language game." The question then becomes, what is the meaning—that is, the use and context—of the concept "knowing" in theological and religious discourse. And it should be added that we may note differences in these contexts as well, between, for example, technical academic theological uses and what Holmer calls the first-order language "of" faith. The additional issue for Holmer is how these two are related, how theology may be properly attentive to and informed by the language of faith.

The Grammar of Faith

As we have noted earlier, in Holmer's view, theology includes both studies about the things of faith and the language of faith itself. The problematic is that theology done in the "about" mood, with its scientific-like language and accompanying notions of rationality and disinterested objectivity, has

117. Ibid.
118. Ibid.

had a kind of ascendancy in the Western tradition that results in its being seen as the paradigm of theological knowing. At the same time, the imagistic, metaphorical and personally expressive discourse of the language of faith is devalued as subjective, irrational and idiosyncratic. But if there is no one standard or single logic for the concept of knowing, then such a hierarchy is not only misdirected but false. For the issue is not lauding emotive, symbolic and expressive language at the expense of objectivity and rationality, but instead recognizing the place and meaning of these latter concepts within the language of faith itself. For on the one hand, as Holmer has stressed time and again, the language of faith is not merely subjective or emotive: "That language does not simply express a way of life, but it, too, becomes extended into a language about everything else in the world."[119] On the other hand, what is said about the context-determined character of the word "knowledge" also applies to such concepts as "objective," "true," "rational," and "real." These criteriological terms always operate with the proviso "in respect to so and so," and therefore, according to Holmer "it is a downright prejudice to believe," for example, "that 'knowledge' has a singular grammar or logic."[120]

What this means for Holmer is that there is simply no across-the-board answer to the question of whether theology is an objective, propositionally-based science. For there are forms of theology, for example, a kind of religious studies that examines the concepts used in theology that can be said to be objective in the same way that we speak about other observational knowledge. In other cases, e.g., the study of the sacraments or the origins and history of doctrines, theology shares features of other historical study. In the same way other kinds of religious studies may be based on the methods and standards of sociological, political or legal disciplines.

But Holmer goes on to distinguish another kind of theology, focused on the language of faith itself. In his view, such study of the language of faith "brings us closer to the actual knowledge of God."[121] It is in attending to this language, its use and grammar, that one comes to discern that "the essence of Christian teaching is available, not just in the commands and assertions

119. Ibid., 189.

120. Ibid., 190. Holmer notes his debt to Wittgenstein and cites his statement in *Philosophical Remarks*, 85: "Philosophy as custodian of grammar can in fact grasp the essence of the world, only not in the propositions of language, but in the rules for this language which excludes nonsensical combinations of signs."

121. Holmer, *Grammar of Faith*, 192.

themselves, but in the rules and grammar of this language."[122] But because it seeks to discern the "grammar" of this language and its use, such study does not limit its examination to the words alone but rather looks to the mode of life in which the language naturally occurs and the situations to which it is addressed.

Holmer is clear, however, that even this language of faith does not impart knowledge of God directly and even "theology as grammar" is no shortcut to knowledge of God; it may be a means to this end, but it is not the thing itself. Rather, in Holmer's terms, there is an additional component at work which distinguishes study of the language of faith from the actual employment of this language: it is, in his terms, obedience and a "simple kind of following": "People become Christian by obeying the first-person language of the Bible and making themselves at home in it."[123]

But because this is the way to real knowledge of God, any theology that fails to take seriously the grammatical import of personal appropriation—what might be called "the logic of obedience"—never approaches the essence of Christianity. First-hand acquaintance with the form of life that makes one a Christian, is, according to Holmer, an essential component of "knowing" the grammar of faith. Whether or not a theologian must himself or herself share in this form of life is left open by Holmer. But in any case, personal acquaintance not only with the doctrines and teachings of the faith but also in some way with what the life of faith consists in— whether affirmed or rejected—would seem to be essential to an authentic understanding of the faith.[124] The limitation of the significance and role of theology, even as a grammar of faith, is important for Holmer both as a way of emphasizing personal knowledge as fundamental to the grammar of faith and as a critique of the presumption of certain theologians and

122. Ibid.

123. Ibid., 193.

124. As we will note in more detail in the next chapter, Holmer suggests Nietzsche and Voltaire as examples of two individuals who do not accept the Christian faith but show in their detailed and nuanced rejection of it, an authentic understanding of what it involves. In reference to Pascal and Voltaire, Holmer comments: "In one sense, both had the grammar straight—one so that he could accept it, the other so that he could at least reject the right thing" (*Grammar of Faith*, 194). A bit earlier Holmer also suggests that perhaps one can come to know the grammar of faith apart from personal appropriation since, in his view: "Even without the latter [first-hand acquaintance with the form of life that makes a person a Christian] the logic and permanent shape of Christianity sometimes begins to shine through the teachings, the modes of life, and the churchly liturgy and practices."

theological systems to displace, and, in some cases, even replace, the first-order language of faith. As Holmer observes in a passage we will quote at some length:

> Such a straightening of thought is about all that theology as grammar can finally do; but from one standpoint, it is quite enough. It tells us what the essence of the matter is, and that can be straightforward, realistic, and true, and not just an opinion. By and large . . . theology is an accounting of how the concepts, including the concept of "God," hang together. One can get the drift of things thereby, and that is not to be made lightly of. But knowing the grammar because of a competence in the language of faith itself is another and profoundly different accomplishment. Perhaps this is like knowing a surface grammar, as a child learns a rule, and a depth grammar, where you cannot state the rule any longer but your conduct bears out the rule at every juncture.[125]

As we have noted, given both the direction and the limitations of theology as the grammar of faith, Holmer suggests that its pedagogical role also has a specific direction and limitation. The difficulties in achieving, or for that matter, communicating, knowledge of God are, in part, what contribute to the continuing generation of "new theologies." From analogy with the empirical sciences and the progression of their underlying conceptualities from the time of the ancients up to the present, the assumption is that theology, too, needs a finer conceptual net with which to grasp divine realities. In the case of both philosophy and theology the application of this analogy translates into the need for new philosophies and theologies based upon them, in order to "state the meanings" of religious language. We have already noted some of the variety of forms such translation may take, but what they share in common, according to Holmer, along with other assumptions about a kind of "infancy of the race" and the presumed ability to better state the meanings of what the ancients "really meant" if they had had the proper conceptual tools, is that there is one way to know a variety of things, "rather than varieties of things to know and appropriate ways to know them."[126]

But whatever the status of such presuppositions—and I believe that Holmer has clearly shown their deficiencies—what amounts to an "artificial" or "invented" language" of many such theologies and a specialized

125. Ibid., 195.
126. Ibid., 197.

vocabulary is not a development of the ordinary language of faith; it therefore does not and, in fact, cannot, serve as the bedrock for Christian faith. This strong rejection applies, for Holmer, at least insofar as such theologies employ new conceptualities and vocabularies in which the nature of God is being re-described so that one can be said to have knowledge of God.[127] In contrast, the concepts of the first-order language of faith are, by and large, not technical; rather, ordinary words are used, but now in particular ways with a grammar that is both describable and public. Words like "hope," "love," "belief," and "grace," for example, are ordinary words, common to everyday parlance; their Christian meaning "comes from the way the term is now bound up with God, on the one hand, and with a world and an individual, on the other."[128] The public character of such terms, when they work as Christian concepts, is that the logic of their use means that one must become hopeful, loving, merciful and the like. If knowledge of God is the issue at stake—as it clearly in for Holmer—then "one must return to the language of faith and think about its province."[129]

The Concept of God

Holmer directly challenges the possibility of "objective knowledge" of God. As he writes: "With objects we have names, and the meaning of names is tied up with the criteria for objects. . . . But with God it makes no sense to ask: 'What is that?' for we do not have access to him as an object such that we can then go on to name."[130] While the notion that God is not an object may meet with a ready agreement, Holmer's contention that "God is not a proper name, either," may be more difficult. But this is, for Holmer, a "grammatical" remark about the word "God." "God is not a name but a concept," Holmer argues, for there "is no such thing as having observational knowledge of God."[131] What Holmer intends by saying God is a concept is that, as we have noted about other concepts understood as "meaning-complexes," the concept of God is taught to us, not merely by learning a definition, but in a variety of concrete practices—through read-

127. Ibid., 198.
128. Ibid., 199.
129. Ibid.
130. Ibid., 200.
131. Ibid., 201–2. Holmer is quoting Kierkegaard when he notes that "God is a concept."

ing Scripture, worship, prayer, and the like—and constitutes an ability or enabling capacity when one masters the rules for the use of the expression. Knowing God—like the case of understanding a concept—is evidenced in the capacities and abilities it enables; one such capacity is the appropriate referring use of the concept of God. And this is the significance of saying that "God is a concept"; namely, not that God is only a concept, but rather that the word *God* is a "descriptive expression" a "kind of accounting" and "predictable term" to which we can refer.

It is within the context of a tradition that includes Scripture and the practice of worship that the concept has this specificity and what it means to understand the concept is shown. In this sense, the concept of God is part of a tradition that precedes the individual knower/believer, just as "the Scripture is an antecedent to our faithful lives."[132] In light of this tradition—which both limits and enables ongoing reflection—theology as the grammar of the faith describes the appropriate uses and connections of the concept. Theology is therefore dependent upon the tradition. As Holmer writes: "Therefore there is a way in which the word *God* comes to mean a great deal for those who are nurtured in the Hebrew-Christian tradition. After a while, one learns who and what that God is, but only by training and exposure. The grammar makes it all manifest. This is why we say again that 'God' is a concept; for to understand the term is to be empowered to think something definite, to be enabled to use the word God in a guarded and responsible sense . . ."[133]

The significance of the tradition for both giving definition to, and providing the context of understanding for, the concept of God is especially important here. For in Holmer's view, apart from the tradition, there is no objective stance by means of which one can judge its proper use. To look for this, as we have noted earlier, is to seek some kind of non-historical, logically-necessary starting point or foundation to secure the practices and perspectives within which the concept *God* has its meaning. As we have seen, for Holmer, the first-order language of faith, and the theology that is its grammar, neither needs nor permits such an external foundation. For there is simply no stance outside of the language of faith which can secure its truth. Once again, if knowing how to use the concept "God" is at least part of what we mean by "knowing God, then "the Bible, the prayer books, the public liturgy, the confessions—these and more are . . . the formats

132. Ibid., 203.
133. Ibid., 205.

within which the knowledge of God is brought to definition."[134] In addition, worship is also the place where what it means to understand the concept is shown. As Holmer writes: "Concepts and ideas are formulated within these matrices, but they are only valid and reliable as religious and Christian ideas if they cause the person to worship God. This is what we mean by getting to know God—namely, that those who know him are those who worship him in spirit and truth.[135]

Within this more circumscribed context, then, theology has both a descriptive and prescriptive role, articulating what Holmer terms "the ruled way, the correct way, of speaking about and worshiping God."[136] Again, theology understood in this way is not a substitute for worship, but like the role of grammar in everyday speech, it informs worship and is, as Holmer emphasizes, "all that we have—namely, knowing what is right to say—and also the way one secures the identity of God. So we do not know the true God or know God truly by a simple use of the word *God*. The true God is known only when his identity is established in a tradition and by a ruled practice of language and worship. This is what the grammar, the theology, provides."[137]

Knowing God

As a way of concluding Holmer goes on to say that rather than a matter of sharing observational knowledge, "knowing God is instead an immediate, non-observational knowledge."[138] In this sense, the context-determined meaning of "knowing God" is akin to knowledge of oneself. As Holmer notes: "The self is not a datum about which one collects evidence. To be a self is to have wants, motives, hopes, and loves. Without these there is nothing to know. The grammar here merges into character."[139] What this means for Holmer is that although God is not an object, it does not follow that the language of faith is not a referring one. Again, because words do not refer by themselves, individuals have to learn to use the language of faith referringly. But the referring use of this expression means the qualification

134. Ibid., 202.
135. Ibid.
136. Ibid., 203.
137. Ibid., 203–4.
138. Ibid., 209.
139. Ibid., 210.

of our own character in such a way that we have a place for God in it; this is the inwardness that Kierkegaard speaks of, and, therefore, to know God, as Holmer puts it, "requires that we become Godly." In this sense, the logically and Christianly proper referring use of the concept *God—what it means to know God*—is that we refer our lives to God. As Holmer writes: "This is what we mean by getting to know God—namely, that those who know him are those who worship him in spirit and truth."[140]

140. Ibid., 202.

4

The Questions of Ontology, Fideism, and Relativism

1. Ontology, Metaphysics, and Theism

To THIS POINT IN our examination we have engaged primarily in a close reading of Holmer's writings and only peripherally considered challenges to the perspectives he forwards. Our intent in this chapter is to consider some critiques of Holmer's thinking, particularly as presented in his *The Grammar of Faith*.

In an article commending Holmer to a wider readership, Patrick Sherry gives a positive response to much of Holmer's philosophical and theological outlook.[1] Sherry recognizes Holmer's fundamental concern with the issue of "learning how" in religious life and his focus with Kierkegaard on the appropriation of Christian faith. He notes, too, the unique character of Holmer's approach to theology and terms his interpretation and use of Wittgenstein's philosophy as "the best attempt made so far to relate Wittgenstein's philosophy to religious issues."[2] Sherry also applauds Holmer's rejection of the idea of "Wittgensteinian" theology and his focus on, what he terms, "spirituality."

However, Sherry takes Holmer to task on a number of points, all of which seem to orbit around what he terms Holmer's "misguided attack"

1. Sherry, "Learning How to Be Religious."
2. Ibid., 82.

on metaphysics. For example, in noting Holmer's rejection of traditional theism as an "academic prejudice," he writes: "It is not surprising that a 'Wittgensteinian' philosophy of religion should have difficulty in accommodating the metaphysical strand in Christian concepts and doctrines. Nevertheless, it is not clear to me that we can dispense with this strand as easily as Holmer thinks we can. If God is indeed a power which can change men's lives, then surely a religious person is committed to an ontology?"[3]

In addition to raising some related issues about the status of theism, Sherry's comments here concerning the necessity of an ontology suggest the more general question of the place of theory in Christian belief. On the one hand, Holmer is arguing that the ordering of such questions is often misperceived: one need not decide the issue of a proper ontology before committing oneself to belief in God. But neither is a theistic conceptual system "in" ordinary religious language. Ontology does not ground religious faith in God. Rather, to the extent we may even use the term "ground," the grounding context for religious faith is confession, prayer, and worship, and corresponding attitudes and orientations, such as a sense of guilt, contriteness of heart, a need for forgiveness and new life. These constitute the "how" that distinguish religious faith from the disinterested entertainment of a proposition about the existence of God. Holmer's view is that a religious belief in God, although it seems, at the least, to imply belief in God's existence, and shares a surface grammar similarity to other hypothetical propositions, is simply not, when its depth grammar is described, equivalent to such a proposition. Moreover, it may be said of theistic or ontological statements that, rather than their being "implied" in religious belief, they have a function and use only in the abstracted language realm of a theistic or ontological scheme. First-order language of faith then neither requires, nor implies, a translation into this other conceptuality.

Holmer's point, with Wittgenstein, is that to remove the language game of "believing in God," from its ordinary context and religious uses to that of the proposition, e.g., "God exists," is to put it in another context with a different operative grammar of "believing," (for example, assenting to the truth of a hypothetical statement or alternatively, believing in the existence of an empirical object), and to put it to a different use. In this sense, the "language game" or "games" of theism and ontology are different than the games of the first-person language of faith.

3. Ibid., 87.

Holmer's critique of theism, then, is both a rejection of the necessity of a metaphysical grounding for religious belief and a critique of its adequacy for expressing either the logic of religious belief or, because of the differences in the use of belief statements in the theistic or ontological game, its actual content. In this sense, what are at stake are both the "how" of religious faith and the "what" of religious beliefs. The statement "God exists" as a statement of theism is neither the same as, nor the foundation for what we mean by "believing in or having faith in God." Religious believers may go on to make statements referring to God, (e.g., the attributes of God), but such assertions neither imply nor necessitate a formal ontology or theistic perspective in the sense of something "standing behind" or implied in the ordinary contextual uses. Indeed, it may be said that the God referred to in a Christian use of the concept is not the same as the theistic use of the concept. As we noted, Holmer argues in the *The Grammar of Faith* that "the referring use of language is not secured by the language itself or some other ratifying ontological scheme;"[4] rather, the speaker does the referring. This in itself may not preclude playing the language games involved in ontology or theism in second-order theology but it recognizes the differences between this and the first-order language uses. And to recognize this difference is to make the issue of theism philosophically gratuitous and religiously trivial.

Yet it may also be said that Holmer is challenging as well the legitimacy of metaphysics and ontology in regard to their self-defined task of organizing concepts into a system. In rejecting the need for, or the meaningfulness of, a system of concepts which somehow stands behind ordinary discourse, as, for example, in regard to the concept "God," Holmer denies the view that there is some pan-logistic perspective that would enable one to relate this concept, in its ordinary usage, to all others uses. One can so define and artificially limit the concept that it will cohere in a system, but this is a different activity than "discovering" some context-independent meaning of the concept. The actual use of such an artificial system for the tasks of theology, even as a second-order discourse, is therefore challenged.

Sherry also argues that for describing and explaining the possibilities of the kind of "religious transformation" that Holmer emphasizes, a religious metaphysics is required, possibly in the form of a model or "projection." He writes: "In the case of Christianity these possibilities are described in terms of the grace of God, i.e., the agency of a transcendent and perfect

4. Holmer, *Grammar of Faith*, 92.

being. Clearly a theologian has his work cut out for him in trying to show that traditional theism is an appropriate model for mankind's religious experience."[5] Without rehashing the arguments we have already noted, I think it may be said that Holmer would simply discount the significance or necessity of the project Sherry outlines. On the one hand, while it is, no doubt, accurate from Holmer's perspective that a "theologian has his work cut out for him" in trying to show the appropriateness of traditional theism, as we have seen, this would apply to any number of theological topics besides religious experience. That is to say, Holmer simply denies the need for a recourse to theism at all. In addition, however, I believe Sherry's criticism illustrates Holmer's argument about a kind of academic prejudice or orientation that calls for an explanatory theory or metaphysical system to account, in this case, for the more ordinary Christian use of the concept of grace. Of course a host of questions might be raised: What is it that requires explanation here, and how would a metaphysical account serve as an explanation? Is it the task of the theologian to provide a general model for "mankind's religious experience?" What purpose would such a model serve? Indeed, is there such a thing as "mankind's religious experience?" Would such a universal model allow for the differences in religious experiences, and what in such a model could count as a substantive difference? What the theologian might properly undertake is a detailed description of the grammar and logic of the concept of grace in Christian religious language. But if it is assumed that a translation into another "more fundamental" conceptual system is required for explanatory purposes, then such a description would be insufficient. And yet the question remains, what more is required and why?

2. Wittgensteinian Fideism and Relatism

Although it is somewhat unfair to Sherry to leave the matter here, and we must note his genuine appreciation for some specific points in Holmer's writings, it seems to me that he exhibits the tendency Holmer speaks of that resists giving up on the idea of metaphysics at any cost. In this case,

---

5. Sherry, "Learning How to Be Religious," 90. Sherry goes on to state: "Moreover, he has to face the difficulty that the God of spiritual light and life is supposed to be the God of Creation and Providence, i.e., he somehow works through nature and history, having cosmological as well as spiritual power. But Holmer's attack on metaphysics seems to me to owe more to an outmoded Positivism than to an appreciation of difficulties."

Wittgenstein's "linguistic turn" simply becomes another theory that allows one to continue to do the same thing. In his "Grammarians and Guardians," D. Z. Phillips notes that Holmer predicted this reaction: "Once a metaphysical view on which, a theologian believes, religion depends comes under attack, that theologian's tendency will be to look for an alternative metaphysical view. It will hardly occur to him or her to locate the confusions in the tendencies of thought which led to the metaphysical view in the first place."[6] It is a similar perspective in a review of Holmer's *The Grammar of Faith* to which we will now turn.

After outlining the strengths and weakness of what he presents as "the four major paradigms in North American theology"—historicized Kantian, process, hermeneutical, and liberation, respectively—Cornel West goes on to list a fifth paradigm which he attributes to Paul Holmer: a "Wittgensteinian-Kierkegaardian paradigm."[7] According to West, Holmer "is one of the few theologians . . . who take seriously the common activities and practices of Christian lay people. . . . to offer a highly plausible philosophical position which puts these activities and practices at the center of theological reflection."[8]

West observes that Holmer's conception of theology "breaks down the modern academic distinctions between theology and preaching, and between theory and practice" and he goes on to suggest that theology "becomes a form of preaching" for "like preaching, theology has an evangelical aim."[9] Although West acknowledges that Holmer does not reduce theology to didactic preaching or move to the other extreme of elevating preaching to propagandistic theology, we may take issue with this notion that theology and preaching are equivalent to one another. As we have noted, Holmer speaks of theology in two different senses, recognizing a second-order language about the faith and a theology, which is more directly in keeping with the first-order language of faith. The aim of *The Grammar of Faith* is to orient theologians to the language of faith and its grammar, but I believe it may be argued that a theology so oriented is still distinguished from the language of faith itself. And although Holmer does say, as West notes, that

---

6. Phillips, "Grammarians and Guardians," 24–25. The following discussion of Cornel West's review of *The Grammar of Faith* is based, in large part, on Phillip's observations in this essay.

7. West, Review of *The Grammar of Faith*, 279–85.

8. Ibid., 281.

9. Ibid.

good preaching is "vernacular theology" and "theology in action," I believe that in the larger context of *The Grammar of Faith*, Holmer is distinguishing theology as a discipline in service to preaching rather than equating it with preaching. This, however, is not a primary point of disagreement.

Where West's comments become problematic—and representative of some of the very problems in contemporary theology that Holmer critiques—is in his assertion that "Holmer's metaphysical assertion is that theology ought to be *part of* the language of the faithful, not *about* this language."[10] To term Holmer's concern that theology focus on description of the language of faith a "metaphysical thesis" strains credulity, but if D. Z. Phillips is correct, this, too, is an instance of the recalcitrance of a metaphysical perspective. As he notes: "As Holmer foresaw, the radical attack of his book can be blunted, if not ignored, by suggesting it, too, offers an alternative metaphysical view . . . We are told: 'Holmer has performed an invaluable service by presenting and promoting a new and exciting viewpoint—the Wittgensteinian-Kierkegaardian paradigm—on the North American theological scene.' The academic practitioners can breathe a sign of relief, a new label has been provided, and now *it* can be discussed."[11] Phillips describes West's attributing of a "new paradigm" to Holmer as a preference for discussing theological labels rather than matters of substance. In addition, Holmer's attack on the alleged foundational status of metaphysics is presented as though it was itself a metaphysical thesis. "In this way," Phillips writes, "the metaphysical game perpetuates itself."[12]

The question before us, then, is whether Holmer's proposal for theology as the "grammar of faith" is a "metaphysical thesis." If we note the theses which West cites—theology "has a participatory dimension which precludes objective, disinterested attempts to 'ground' that language of the faithful in some ontology, metaphysics or upon some set of 'undeniable facts'"; theology "must always move toward a present-tense, first-person mood"; theology "sets forth the structure of Christian faith or the rules and grammar of the life and language of the faithful with 'the form of personal appropriation built in'"—we may ask, in what sense are these assertions "metaphysical"?

10. Ibid. Although Phillips responds to this same assertion on West's part about Holmer's "metaphysical thesis," one cannot help but wonder if this was a typographical error that was meant instead to read "Holmer's anti-metaphysical thesis." The balance of West's article, however, does not bear out this interpretation.

11. Phillips, "Grammarians and Guardians," 25.

12. Ibid., 26.

To the extent that Holmer is arguing the case for a particular under-standing of the purpose and proper method of theology it might be argued that he is making something akin to a general statement about the scope and method of an entire field of inquiry. In addition, his interpretation and use of the writings of Kierkegaard and Wittgenstein may be viewed as promoting a different paradigm for theology. Whether it is Holmer's in-tent to "promote" a paradigm may be debated, but this, of course, need not preclude one characterizing it in this way. Yet from our survey of Holmer's thought it should be clear that the influence of Kierkegaard and Wittgen-stein has more to do with a "way" of thinking than with the promulgation of an alternative theoretical content for theology. Although Kierkegaard may be said to have a "theory" of the self (e.g., the spheres of existence) it serves a descriptive and pedagogical rather than explanatory function, and the same may be said for his theory of "indirect communication." In the case of Wittgenstein's analytic philosophy there is a clear orientation away from generalization and speculation towards concrete examples and description.

Holmer's argument that the proper theological task is a descriptive rendering of the grammar of faith is itself forwarded on the basis of a de-scriptive analysis of the distinctive grammar and logic of the language of faith, and is therefore a call for a way of doing theology which is appropri-ate to its subject matter. What might be termed "presuppositions" include the idea that subject matter of theology is the distinctive content of the Christian faith and that theology serve preaching, the practices of the life of faith and the promulgation of the gospel. In light of this it is argued that attention must be given to the appropriation of the faith and the activities that nurture and form the life of faith. But again, these are not promoted as trans-field theoretical proposals but instead as observations, which either show or fail to show their adequacy in light of the content and significance of Christian belief. In the same way, Holmer's critiques of contemporary theology, of theism and ontology either make their case or fail to on the basis of their accuracy of description rather than requiring a prior assent to an underlying conceptual scheme.

The same may be said, I believe, in regard to what West terms Holmer's "controversial philosophical views on truth, objectivity, rationality, and va-lidity." These views may indeed be "controversial," but West's contention that Holmer's conception of theology merely "presupposes" such "views" fails to recognize that in the course of *The Grammar of Faith* Holmer also demonstrates the case for what he says about the context-dependent character of these concepts.

Holmer's proposal "may" be taken as a theoretical proposition, but it is clear, I believe, that it is not raised or argued in this manner. Rather, the idea of theology as the grammar of faith is forwarded itself as an analytical description of the internal logic and grammar of the theological enterprise. There are no grand claims made or requirements for theology as a whole to adopt a new conceptual system. It is, however, clearly a methodological proposal—a way of "doing" theology—and may be debated on these terms. In this sense, then, while Holmer's notion of theology as the grammar of faith is in no way a metaphysical thesis, it may be treated as a theoretical proposal pertaining to theological methodology. This is to say that Holmer's claim to be offering a "descriptive" rendering is not, in itself, proof of the claim. Demonstration of the appropriateness of this understanding of theology to its subject matter and the usefulness of its methodological orientation are the ways to determine this.

In regard to the idea of a "Wittgensteinian-Kierkegaardian" paradigm, we may reiterate the perspective that it is not Holmer's intent to promote a new paradigm, but rather to learn from both Kierkegaard and Wittgenstein, among others, those ways of thinking that attend to the connection of language and life, that focus on concrete examples and the descriptive rendering of these examples and that resist the impulse toward generalization and system-building. This perspective may serve as a paradigm, but unless such naming serves as a motivation for one to actually do theology in this way, Holmer's purpose is not forwarded by it. In any event, as we noted earlier, D. Z. Phillips observes that another label has already "beaten it in consumer appeal," namely, "Wittgensteinian fideism."[13]

The designation of "Wittgensteinian fideism" has been coined in response to what are seen to be the relativistic implications of Wittgenstein's notion of "language games" and "forms of life." The argument is that Wittgenstein has divided language into distinct and autonomous compartments that then makes it impossible to critique a particular language game except from within the form of life of which it is part. If one does not share this form of life—in this case, religious faith—it is argued that there is no possibility of a criticism of religious faith. The alleged result is that language games and the forms of life of which they are part are insulated from one

---

13. Ibid., 25. The origin of the term "Wittgensteinian fideism" is usually credited to Kai Nielsen, in his "Wittgensteinian Fideism."

another, preventing any real debate or an appeal to a shared standard outside of the differing language games and forms of life for judging issues of truth and falsity.

West raises some of these criticisms of *The Grammar of Faith*, noting that Holmer's viewpoint "raises unsurprising accusations of relativism, skepticism and even 'closet' nihilism."[14] He asks whether "contextualism" is not a form of relativism and wonders if truth is contextual how do we know what really *is*? But West goes on to answer his own questions by noting that Holmer's aim is "to rid us of this 'really-disease,'" by forcing us to look at the world as fallen, finite human beings rather than presuming a God's-eye view. While we need not respond to each of the questions raised by West, it is important to suggest a general response to these allegations of fideism and relativism.

D. Z. Phillips notes one response to the issues raised when he cites Holmer's discussion of whether someone who does not share a Christian form of life can adequately understand the faith. Holmer notes that "it is conceivable that a theologian can describe a lot of what he or she might not intimately share," and then goes on to suggest the examples of Nietzsche and Voltaire as understanding but rejecting the faith:

> Nietzsche's aversion to Christianity was so profound and so detailed that his pages outline a faith in Jesus that is worthy of offense. For this reason, his work helps us to see how blessed someone is who is not offended by Jesus. Nietzsche understood but was antipathetic. Voltaire's conception that Pascal's account of Christianity is misanthropic suggests that both Voltaire and Pascal had seen the logic of faith correctly. In one sense, both had the grammar straight—one so that he could accept it, the other so that he could at least reject the right thing.[15]

According to Phillips, Holmer's depiction represents a genuine clash of the counter-claims of truth and falsity. This example suggests that there is the possibility of real disagreement whether or not one shares a religious form of life. Such genuine disagreement is, however, contingent upon one actually having an accurate account of the faith to which one can respond. The task of theology is to get this grammar straight; doing this, however, does not guarantee that one will come to accept the faith so described. In

---

14. West, Review of *The Grammar of Faith*, 283.

15. Holmer, *Grammar of Faith*, 194. Also cited in Phillips, "Grammarians and Guardians," 28.

Holmer's view, there simply is no such guarantee, and the presumption of theism, or any other metaphysical system, to furnish one is false. As Holmer asks, "Isn't this all the nearer to faith any third-person account can bring us?"[16] Moreover, it is the traditional reliance on such metaphysical schemes for providing the ground and "meaning" of religious faith that, in fact, raises the specter of skepticism and relativism. In reference to the various systems into which the first-order language of Christian faith is translated, Holmer argues, "each system seems to work well as one reads it, but the next one does equally well. Skepticism ensues, for there is no outside domain, no context in which such expressions have a genuine and useful role."[17] And while there is no context-free, pan-logistic standard to arbitrate disputes and determine what is "really" the case, there is both the possibility of persuasion (or, perhaps, conversion is the better term) and the ordinary context of human life in which persons may be moved either to choose or to reject religious faith.

Although our survey of Holmer's writings has not dealt with this directly, in Holmer's interpretation and application of Wittgenstein's notions of "language games" and "forms of life," there are no hard and fast definitions or precise delineations given that would require the isolation or complete autonomy of either language games or forms of life. Moreover, in Holmer's usage, the language "of" faith, although clearly connected to a religious "form of life," does not consist in one, distinct language game, but a variety of games. Like Wittgenstein, Holmer presents no definite "theory" of language games or forms of life. Instead these notions serve as a kind of reminder to look at the uses of expressions and the larger context of the life in which they ordinarily occur.

A final critique that West notes is that Holmer is "neither Wittgensteinian or Kierkegaardian enough."[18] While one might think that this would undermine the view that Holmer promotes a Kierkegaardian–Wittgensteinian paradigm, West instead raises the more substantive issue of what he views to be Holmer's "conservative" reading of Kierkegaard and Wittgenstein evidenced in his downplaying the uncertainty of faith and his attempt to "freeze" the rules and grammar of the language of faith. Although he does not address it directly, these concerns also give entry to the question of

---

16. Holmer, *Grammar of Faith*, 194.

17. Ibid., 199.

18. West, Review of *The Grammar of Faith*, 283.

whether Holmer's polemic against what he views as theological novelty—what he terms "journalistic theology"—is overstated.

We may respond to the first issue in regard to Kierkegaard by noting that, at least in the context of *The Grammar of Faith*, it may be argued that Holmer need not further stress the "objective uncertainty" of faith because he has already done this in pushing away the props of metaphysical foundations and rejecting attempts to either "ground" the faith or verify its beliefs by reference to a context-free, omniscient perspective. Given the risk that religious faith involves and the difficulty in commending this faith, in his focus on theology as grammar, the logic of Christian concepts and their appropriation, Holmer's concern is that it is, in fact, the gospel message that one is confronted with rather than a second-order ideology posing as the Christian faith. But if one is presented with the authentic Christian message, because of the "what" of the Christianity and the "how" of faith, Kierkegaard's "leap of faith" is still necessary.

West also criticizes Holmer's failure to recognize the heterogeneity of the Christian tradition and the fact that the very religious language and practices that Holmer sees as fundamental to the faith are being called into question. Here Holmer is seen as not being sufficiently "Wittgensteinian" and West views Holmer's use of the expressions as "the Christian Scripture," and "the liturgy" as based on the presumption of an organic, cohesive tradition. What this indicates to West is that Holmer has failed to recognize the way that the language of faith and its grammar are part of the flux of human history and therefore open to change. D. Z. Phillips also wonders about the situation of the primary language of faith "becoming increasingly unavailable because the well is poisoned at its source."[19] Both West and Phillips raise an important question about the loss of a shared understanding of the language, practices and life of faith. What is Holmer's response?

In our earlier chapter focusing on his understanding and use of Wittgenstein's later philosophical analysis we noted some aspects of Holmer's response to the "problem of religious language" and its alleged loss of meaning as represented by John Robinson's *Honest to God* and the "death of God" discussion of the 1960s.[20] But I believe it may be argued that what Holmer is doing in *The Grammar of Faith* as a whole is his response. With Wittgenstein, Holmer sees the importance of understanding religious

19. Phillips, "Grammarians and Guardians," 30.

20. Holmer, "Language and Theology," in *Grammar of Faith*, 241–61; *Grammar of Faith*, 112–35.

language and beliefs as they come to us out of a long tradition of beliefs, practices and the conventions of a community of faith interwoven in such a way that they form the lives of those who participate in them. With Kierkegaard Holmer is concerned with "learning how to be religious," with the individual and the modification of self-understanding that religious faith requires and nurtures. It is the interaction between, and what he sees as the necessary correlation of, a larger tradition of beliefs and practices with the subjectivity of the individual that Holmer outlines in his analysis of the language of faith. And it is here that his concerns that the particular grammar of the language of faith not be displaced or lost in a maze of conflicting second-order schemes and that theological reflection aid the task of Christian nurture meet.

That is to say, Holmer may not emphasize the heterogeneity of the Christian tradition or the breakdown of a shared community of belief and practice, but this is the case, I believe, because it is precisely this situation that he seeks to address in his call for theology to be the grammar of faith, to, in a sense, return to its roots in primary, shared and enduring religious language and practice, in Scripture and tradition. As we will further explore in the next chapter, along with C. S. Lewis, Holmer believes there is a basic core of Christianity represented by the kerygma, the teachings and the creeds that is not, or at the least, need not, function as a second-order interpretation. It is the work of theology as the grammar of faith to reflect on this core and to guard against the importation of extraneous interpretations. D. Z. Phillips notes this when he speaks of Holmer's "evangelical intent." He goes on to write: "When we read *The Grammar of Faith*, it is clear that Holmer is doing far more than informing himself and his audience of theology's proper task. He is also engaged *in* the task himself. Holmer not only informs, he also incites. Holmer says that when he does his work properly, the Christian teacher, the theologian, dares to become the guardian of the language of faith."[21]

It is this role as "guardian" of the faith, as well as "grammarian" that underlies Holmer's larger theological project. And it is here that we may say that Holmer moves beyond the purely descriptive work of the philosopher to a "prescriptive" task as Christian theologian. In this sense, Holmer's response to the situation described by West and Phillips is no one argument, but rather, the whole of his work as philosopher and theologian.

---

21. Phillips, "Grammarians and Guardians," 34.

What we are suggesting, then, is that Holmer is motivated by a practical concern. The use of the term "practical" is not intended in the disparaging way that it is sometimes used to distinguish the supposedly mundane concerns of practical theology from the higher, more intellectual concerns of systematic theology. Rather, it is meant to reflect Holmer's rejection of the whole theory/practice bifurcation of matters and the concomitant rejection of the view that abstract and theoretical pursuits are somehow more significant, deeper and more profound than a focus on the ordinary language and practice of faith. This is not to forward yet another theory; rather, it is to recognize, as Holmer does, the expansiveness of the concept of rationality as applied to different concerns and fields of inquiry. It is both to accept the limits of knowledge and to be rigorous and clear in the kind of reflection that is appropriate to the logic of the Christian faith. For theology, then, it is to explore the "rationality," the logical pattern, in the grammatical interconnection of the "what" of Christian belief and the "how" of subjective appropriation.

And where the descriptive and prescriptive tasks meet in Holmer's combining of the perspectives of Wittgenstein and Kierkegaard is an understanding of the language of faith and its connection to the development of a Christian form of life. It may be said, as Phillips suggests, that Holmer presents a kind of epistemology of religion, exploring the grammar of the interconnection of the Christian faith, its teachings and practices, with the individual. For, as we have seen, like Kierkegaard, Holmer sees a life informed by ethical and Christian concepts as essential to the development of an abiding sense of self; and with Wittgenstein, Holmer explores the grammar of religious language and belief which links understanding and personal appropriation. The meeting place, then, is the human personality, the self. But given the connotations of the term "self" in Western intellectual history—isolated and autonomous, the ground of knowledge and certainty—its use here may be misleading. Because what Holmer is talking about is not an isolated intellect but the whole person, in community, linked to a tradition of beliefs and practices. For this reason, another term is more appropriate: it is "character." For what Holmer seeks to describe and aid is the development of a distinctive Christian character. It is to this last subject we now turn.

5

Making Christian Sense

> "To know the grammar of life is like knowing the grammar of a living language; it enables and empowers one to make sense."[1]

1. Introduction

IN THIS CONCLUDING CHAPTER our intent is to present a summary view of some of the fundamental themes of Holmer's thought and to assess his overall contribution to contemporary theology and philosophy. As a way of contextualizing our consideration of these matters, we will look at two works in Holmer's corpus that we have not yet discussed, namely, his *C. S. Lewis: The Shape of His Faith and Thought* and *Making Christian Sense*. In both these works Holmer articulates a view of the relation of ethics to the Christian faith, a "morality of the virtues" and character, and addresses some important theological issues in a manner that might be termed "first-person." These two books provide an insight into the practical and personal import of Holmer's more scholarly philosophical and theological writings.

It is this last title, in particular, that may serve as a kind of summary statement of Paul L. Holmer's unique contribution to Christian theology. For what Holmer says of Lewis in his *C. S. Lewis: The Shape of His Faith and Thought* applies equally to his own thought, namely, "that all of us are in need of making sense of ourselves, our thoughts and our behavior and

1. Holmer, *Making Christian Sense*, 73.

that both morals and Christianity [speak] to that plain condition."[2] I believe it may be said that what Paul Holmer is about in the whole of his writings is a careful articulation of what is involved in "making sense" of our lives, personally, morally and religiously.

In the introduction to his *The Grammar of Faith* Holmer states that the purpose of his work is to articulate "a morphology of the life of Christian belief." As we have noted in earlier chapters, this notion of mapping the logic and grammar of Christian belief suggests the influence of both Kierkegaard and Wittgenstein and how the perspectives of these two thinkers converge in Holmer's writings. For as Kierkegaard in his "stages" charts the general options available to human subjectivity he also suggests the "logic" of these stages or spheres of existence, the way that emotions and passions and all else that constitutes human subjectivity have a kind of internal ordering and sense. Kierkegaard also emphasizes the necessary correlation of the "how" of faith—faith as passionate appropriation—with the "what" or the content of the Christian faith. This correlation of subject and object is part of the "logic" of Christian belief. It is the descriptive rendering of this same logic that Holmer is concerned to articulate in his own "morphology of belief," motivated by a similar interest to make sense of the seemingly incoherent machinations of the self, in order to show the possibilities of growth in self-understanding and the character of religious faith. All this is noted as well within the context of ordinary life, in the realm of what is accessible to and incumbent upon all persons. And it is this same concern to articulate the ruled connections of language and life, again in the context of the everyday and ordinary, that Holmer discerns in Wittgenstein's reflections. It is in keeping with this perspective that Holmer proceeds to articulate a view of theology as "the grammar of faith."

Here the orientation to close description of the activity of speaking and how this activity is woven into a form of life becomes another tool for showing the order and logic of self-understanding as it is formed by ethical and religious concepts and the practices in which they are born and manifested. Here "understanding" has a necessary connection to how one lives, and the movement toward greater self-understanding is evidenced in the formation of character and definition in one's life. The concept of "grammar," then, includes not simply the ordering of words and concepts, but the connection of language to life, the way that ethical and religious language is connected to, and forms, a life. It is this extension of the concepts

2. Holmer, *C. S. Lewis*, 3.

of logic and grammar to the project of making sense with, and of, one's life that Holmer suggests when he writes: "Just as having a grammar in our language helps us to make sense with our words, so, too, having a grammar of our emotions, or our will, or our moral action helps us make sense of our lives."[3]

2. Making Sense

Early on in his *Making Christian Sense*, Holmer writes that his purpose in this work concerns the "pragmatics, the common ways in which all of us have to make use of Christian teachings."[4] I believe that it may be said that this sense of "pragmatics" and "making use" of the Christian teachings is at the heart of Holmer's theological reflection as a whole. For even in his most analytic writings, his concern is with understanding the lived experience of the faith, the life of faith, and the way Christian concepts and teachings find their place in the context of human life. And in Holmer's view, these teachings and the way of life they enable and require, find linkage in a common human condition and experience. It is this concern with the individual human self, regardless of the specifics of time and place, that he sees addressed by Kierkegaard in his charting of human subjectivity. Concerning this universal aspect of the human condition, Holmer quotes Samuel Johnson's observation:

> We are all prompted by the same motives, all deceived by the same fallacies, all animated by the same hope, obstructed by danger, entangled by desire, and seduced by pleasure . . .The main of life is, indeed, composed of small incidents and petty occurrences: of wishes for objects not remote and grief for disappointments of no fatal consequences, of insect vexations . . . Such is the general heap out of which every man is to cull his own condition. . . .[5]

It is a similar perspective that Holmer notes in C. S. Lewis' writings on both the condition that Christianity addresses and the critical and polemic form it must take: "Therefore, anything germane to the loves, hopes, wants of mankind in one age are probably appropriate now too. The need is always

---

3. Holmer, *Making Christian Sense*, 73.

4. Ibid., 21.

5. Samuel Johnson, *The Rambler*, Essays #60 and #68, quoted in Holmer, *C. S. Lewis*, 4.

to break through the conventional framework of current thinking that will otherwise keep us shallow and trivial.[6]

This concern with the pragmatics, the "how" of the development of a distinctive Christian consciousness and life, is also at the heart of Holmer's critique of contemporary theology. For as we have seen in the *Grammar of Faith*, and as he reiterates in *Making Christian Sense*, Holmer is critical of a "vast and technical literature" that details the "what" of Christian teachings but fails to address the "how" of them. And this concern, as we have seen, is not merely that of "application" but the philosophical critique of a way of doing theology that fails to recognize the importance of the first-order language of faith and the meaning-context of religious language and belief provided by the practices of the life of faith.

In addition, it is not simply that this technical literature fails to contextualize the faith, but that it comes to stand between believers and the practice of faith, as though one must first master this material, "choose" a theology among the myriad of competitors, before one can proceed with the more ordinary, and yet much more demanding, practice of being faithful. Again, Holmer notes a similar critique in C. S. Lewis' writings when he writes: "Lewis shows us how a very shallow kind of mentality develops, oftentimes in universities and public life. Soon an easy and plausible synthesis of science and current attitudes gives it a kind of status. The complicity of ourselves with the thought of the day will often mean that the psychomania, that dramatic inner life to which we are entitled, will be omitted."[7]

All of this stands behind Holmer's concern for "building up" a "Christian mind" by "fashioning distinctive Christian emotions, by considering new virtues, by finding a new power and shape for the will and also by making a kind of sense in thought and belief."[8] And the "building up" that Holmer seeks here suggests that kind of "edification" that Kierkegaard promoted in his own religious discourses. For just as Holmer characterizes Kierkegaard's *Edifying Discourses* as attempts "to stimulate and also to discipline our feelings, wishes and hopes," so *Making Christian Sense* may, I believe, be characterized as Holmer's own "edifying discourse."[9] And al-

---

6. Holmer, *C. S. Lewis*, 17.

7. Ibid.

8. Holmer, *Making Christian Sense*, 20.

9. The third volume in The Paul L. Holmer Papers, *Communicating the Faith Indirectly*, contains essays, sermons, and occasional pieces that also might fit this designation of "edifying discourse."

though Holmer's work is clearly Christian in orientation, he shares with Kierkegaard the intent to address a universal human condition of lostness and despair and the conviction that "every man is potentially a being of spirit," that "the awakening of inwardness is the beginning of the relationship to God."[10]

Throughout his *Making Christian Sense* Holmer also addresses the question of the relation of ethics to Christian faith, most particularly in his discussion of the virtues. As he writes, for example: "Despite big differences between morality and Christianity, the fact is that both are also disciplines that aim at providing a cure for the lack of emotions as well as a pattern for new emotions."[11] The question of in what these similarities and differences consist is an important one. For, on the one hand, following Kierkegaard's lead, Holmer recognizes sharp distinctions between an ethical versus a distinctively Christian way of life. On the other hand, Holmer clearly sees an ethical consciousness as preparatory for Christian faith, and writes that making sense morally is a "minimum natural requirement" to making sense Christianly.[12] But he also argues that a life formed and characterized by the ethical concern and the virtues is necessarily part of the Christian way of life. From within the perspective of theology as the grammar of faith and Holmer's "morphology of the life of Christian belief," the question then becomes, what is the relation between morality and religious faith? This, in turn, raises the traditional Christian question of the role of grace in the life of faith? Given Holmer's emphasis on what might be termed the "behavioral" consequences of religious belief in light of Wittgenstein's connection of meaning and use, and his rejection of a "mentalist" picture of understanding for one that emphasizes the way that understanding is "shown" in one's life, how do the Christian concepts of grace, forgiveness and the Reformation emphasis on *simul justus et peccator* figure in? It is my view that both Holmer's *Making Christian Sense* and his *C. S. Lewis: The Shape of His Faith and Thought* help to clarify these questions. The fact that they both do this in the context of the personal and practical meaning, that is, in reference to the "how" of faith, and do so by presenting a paradigm of character development, suggests part of the answer as well.

10. Holmer, "Introduction," in Kierkegaard, *Edifying Discourses*, viii.

11. Holmer, *Making Christian Sense*, 24.

12. Ibid., 75.

3. The Virtues

Holmer observes that the very idea of the virtues has largely gone out of style in an age which values individuality and self-expression above all else. He argues, however, that this is not a uniquely modern phenomenon and, as noted earlier, that the situation the virtues speak to is not limited to a particular culture or time: "Courage, temperance and justice are not just accidental points of view, useful for one time and not for another. They are not relative or pertinent to just one society, one epoch, or one culture. Instead they are needed because of the way that people always are and the ways social and physical contexts are."[13] Holmer does not see this as a theoretical or an *a priori* claim, but simply a description of the workings of human interaction and life. In the end, according to Holmer, if we pay attention to our own lives, to the conflicts we face and the judgments we make upon ourselves, we will begin to discover "the plain truth, that we are moral beings."[14]

In a similar way, Holmer observes that the Bible addresses this situation of conflict and self-judgment when it speaks about the need for justification. It is significant in Holmer's view that the Bible doesn't engage in argumentation around this issue, but instead "the common human situation that one requires a life that is right and righteous, that is happy and justifiable, is simply assumed."[15] This does not mean that no grounds can be offered, but it is an important theological point to observe that the justification of this view does not come first; there is no need for a theory or grounding in order to understand the situation Scripture addresses. Holmer writes that "the Bible would not speak to the human condition at all if it were not that each person can discover for himself or herself this need for rightness. The Bible . . . is made for seekers, for sojourners, for those who need justification and validity. And part of its content is plainly moral, telling us how laws and commands can meet the indigence of the human spirit."[16]

As Holmer sees it, conceived and articulated in view of this universal human situation, there is a similar lack of need of justification for the virtues. For, as he writes, "the virtues simply recommend themselves. They

13. Ibid., 69.
14. Ibid., 62.
15. Ibid., 63.
16. Ibid.

need no case made for them at all. They are not part of a point of view";
rather than justification, however, they may require something else on the
part of a person, for whether "one is attracted to them or not depends upon
the way one's emotions, wants and feelings have been trained."[17]

In this sense, then, although the virtues address a common human situation, they are not a natural proclivity but must be acquired and learned.
Because the virtues correlate with the unpredictable nature of events and
circumstances confronting human beings, an essential feature of a virtue
is the ordering of a "predictability" or "proneness" in behavior. As Holmer
defines virtue: "What we mean by a virtue, then, is an acquired disposition
or inclination that will make behavior predictable and regular."[18] The virtues, in this sense, are "standing capacities" and organized "ways of coping"
with an uncertain world and consist in the disposition or tendency to act
in a certain way.

Because of the apparent contradictions of their opposites, the vices, to
live with the concepts of justice, courage and temperance is also to discern
something of the way life is. As Holmer writes: "It is downright folly when
we believe that all standards are individual and that everyone's life is an
essay into the morally unknown. On the contrary, who with a clear thought
and awareness of himself or herself could ever choose to be cowardly?"[19] It
is in light of their connection with "the way things are with all of us" that to
endorse virtues and eschew vices is to learn something of "the grammar of
life." As Holmer writes: "But virtues and vices are already there as a big part
of the grammar of life. . . . to know the grammar of life is like knowing the
grammar of a living language; it enables and empowers one to make sense.
In fact, it does not tell us what to do any more than English grammar tells
us what to say, but it does tell us *how* to live just as the constructions of a
language inform us *how* to express ourselves."[20]

17. Holmer, *C. S. Lewis*, 54.

18. Holmer, *Making Christian Sense*, 67.

19. Ibid., 71–72. In "Making Sense Christianly," a baccalaureate sermon recently
published in *Communicating the Faith Indirectly*, Holmer makes a similar observation
about the universality of the virtues: "It is an egregious error to hold that all morals are
subjective or only a matter of being conditioned. We go beyond the limits of any kind of
understanding if we should choose to be cowardly. And the person who lapses into despair and who loses all notion of anything mattering is certainly in need of hope. By the
same token, hope, courage, and temperance belong to the very marrow of our humanity,
and we are not free to eschew them" (137).

20. Holmer, *Making Christian Sense*, 73.

Holmer also sees something more in the virtues, for in the way they change one's perceptions and orientation, their "habitual" character begins to form the life of one who practices them. In this sense, the virtues also serve an educatory function. Becoming moral is a kind of education in itself, involving the development of hopes and cares, wants and desires, and also the ability to discern and order these. To live with the virtues, then, is to be changed by them and to be moved "into a new way of thinking and living, and even perceiving the world."[21] It is for this reason that C. S. Lewis viewed the moral requisites as "schoolmasters preparing us for becoming Christians."

It is this last remark about the role of morality, as stated elsewhere as the "minimum natural requirement" for understanding Christian teachings, together with the emphasis on the importance of a life ordered by the virtues as necessary for making sense of one's life, that may raise questions about the ordering of ethics and Christian faith, the role of the will, and the traditional issue of "grace versus works." Holmer is quite aware of these concerns, however, and addresses them directly.

He notes, for example, that while secular moralists and Christians might agree on the debilitating effects of a wounded conscience, Christians add to the requirement of moral reform the need for a forgiveness that only God can give. For as Holmer recognizes, there is a particular difficulty to moral striving that Christian literature emphasizes and addresses: "We are prone to think we can establish ourselves in righteousness and that we can overcome the wasting and gnawing sense of not being good enough by moral effort. . . . But Christian teaching tells us plainly that doing the works of the law will not establish our righteousness.[22] Holmer does not intend to displace the Lutheran concept of "forensic" justification, speaking of the story of Jesus Christ as portraying a passive or imputed righteousness received from God, "a righteousness that is given and not achieved."[23] He is equally clear about the ordering of grace and works, as this order is related to the theological concepts of justification and sanctification. As he observes: "Certainly we have to avoid the notion that being a Christian is a matter of works, even a matter of doing this or that and making something of oneself. Instead, faith, even belief, comes first, and the works follow."[24]

21. Holmer, *C. S. Lewis*, 101.
22. Holmer, *Making Christian Sense*, 76.
23. Ibid., 77.
24. Ibid., 29.

But Holmer also stresses that the God of the law and the God of Jesus Christ are the same God. And he argues that Luther's notion of an "active righteousness" and faith active in love are essential to the Christian understanding of the meaning of faith and faithfulness. While the Christian is still called to make sense of his or her life, and therefore, morality and the virtues still have a role, the essential difference for the Christian is that the motivation and goal of the virtuous life are re-described. As he writes: "The motive for becoming virtuous and good no longer has to be to please God or even to please oneself. . . . once one is a Christian, the works become a consequence of the new confidence, the new certainty, and the new righteousness that faith provides. . . . We need no longer be in despair even if we fail, for the Christian gospel is the story of God's love which justifies us when we truly believe and trust God, not just when we succeed morally."[25]

In this sense, the Christian no longer requires that moral effort bear the burden of being salvific, but it is precisely this reorienting of the issue that allows the virtues to assume their proper role of providing a dispositional regularity and order in one's life. When released from the burden of self-justification, "it is as if we are free of having to use morals for non-moral ends."[26] Indeed, it can be said that the moral life shows its preparatory function in making us aware of our need for a forgiveness we cannot give ourselves when we despair at our inability to justify our lives. It may even be said that the "accusatory" function of Luther's "second use" of the law is not overturned, despite Holmer's emphasis on the virtues.

It is both the preparatory character of the virtues, the notion that making sense morally is "something like a minimum natural requirement" for understanding Christian teaching and the centrality of moral teaching within the Christian faith that underlies the critique of the absence of these concerns from much contemporary Christian theology. Holmer contends that "it is an omission among Christian thinkers if the new life in Christ is not also conceived as a new way to make sense, even morally."[27] In another context, Holmer argues that religious teaching becomes no more than a "playful abstraction" if we forget the ways that a person is formed and nurtured by means of ethical concern. It is this perspective that suggests another and deeper significance to the ethical life, both as a preparation for, and as an embodiment of, religious faith. It is the claim that a life formed

25. Ibid., 78.
26. Ibid.
27. Ibid., 28.

by ethical concepts, connected to a wider community of meaning and practice, is essential to developing the capacity for belief in God. This, in turn, is linked to an understanding of the Christian faith not seen primarily as a set of doctrines, but as "a way," a life, so that it may be said that despite the "big differences between morality and Christianity, the fact is that both are disciplines . . ."[28] And intimately connected to this, then, is a description of the formation of persons that focuses on the "how" of ethical and religious thought and life. But in order to see this, another kind of thinking and another view of Christianity must be critiqued.

4. Contra the Theories

Holmer forwards a view of the moral life which, at least according to his argument, is not dependent upon the prior acceptance of a theory of ethics. This is a perspective he attributes to C. S. Lewis when he suggests the following example: "Think for a moment about the person who is trustworthy and honest, perhaps also favored with a confidence and hope in God. How tempting it is to 'construe' such a person as 'believing' in God or 'believing in the general good' and leave things there. Ethicists after a while lose touch with the specific likings, animosities, disappointments, griefs, odd wants, that persuade this person that he had better keep himself trustworthy or else he could not make much sense of anything."[29] Holmer's point is that it is a mistake of what he terms "moral theory talk" to "construe" matters in such a way that assent to a moral theory or general law is attributed when, in his view, the individual characteristics of the person—not accidental, but long-term concerns and wants and commitments—are what are exemplified. Again, as he attributes to Lewis: "Moral culture is not a matter of fitting particulars to universals, or subsuming instances in one's personal life to general laws; instead it involves the actual development of wants and desires, hopes and cares and the capacities to judge them in a variety of ways."[30] Holmer is not contesting any particular ethical theory here, but

---

28. Ibid., 24.

29. Holmer, *C. S. Lewis*, 53. The recently published *Thinking the Faith with Passion*, 304–20, includes a previously unpublished essay, "The Case for the Virtues." In addition to supplementing Holmer's discussion of the virtues in *Making Christian Sense*, as the editors of the collection note, "Holmer investigates 'virtue ethics' as an important corrective over against much ethical theorizing" (xv).

30. Holmer, *C. S. Lewis*, 53.

rather the mind set that assumes a theory must be operative, that it is explanatory in a way superior to a more informal description, and that the generalization a theory makes possible is its superior explanatory power. We have previously noted something of this critique in Holmer's reading of Kierkegaard and at various points in his *The Grammar of Faith*. But here we wish to connect the critique of theory-language to Holmer's understanding of the Christian faith, the human person and the points of connection between the two.

In the thought of C.S. Lewis Holmer sees this more general rejection of the insistent presumption that one must have a theory at work before one can make a rational decision or judgment in the fields of literature or ethics or in regard to the Christian faith. According to Holmer, Lewis argued that "theories were not the fundamental subject matter, either in great literature, for making a life virtuous, or for becoming a Christian," and in place of this, "forged a conception of what theories and people were such that the logic of indecision, of relativism, of countless incompatibles was bypassed altogether."[31] For his own part Holmer sees in the viewpoint that emphasizes the primacy of theory a particular conception of "rationality" which defines the issue in such a way that "being rational" comes to be synonymous with having an explicit theory by which one makes judgments. But at least in the realms of aesthetics, ethics and religion, when one is presented with competing theories and world views the result is simply an ever-retreating possibility of certainty and a postponement of judgment or action. Holmer gives the example of a scientific outlook to suggest the way that its description of atoms and the like is appropriate within its field, but the hypotheses of science and this language of atoms and molecules do not displace, nor can they properly displace, our ordinary ways of speaking and interacting with chairs or other solid physical objects. Where the significant conflict between such different ways of describing things comes to the fore is when the question, "But what is the world really?" is asked and we suppose that words like "real" and "true" and others are somehow univocal and definitive in all contexts. With Lewis, however, Holmer argues against this "legislative assumption" of a general or theoretical outlook: "But surely, there is no right in popular fashion, or for that matter a science, or a religion, or a peculiar philosophical outlook, of determining once and for all

---

31. Ibid., 23.

the meanings of 'real' or 'true'. That is what happens if a theory, philosophical or otherwise, begins to legislate."[32]

As we have suggested, Holmer sees the same assumptions about the univocality of "rationality" and alleged trans-field concepts like "real" and "truth" at work in the various theoretical proposals that constitute a major theme in contemporary Christian theology. But applying the same critical perspective that he sees in C. S. Lewis, he argues that religious belief does not consist in choosing, for example, for or against a particular Christology or ecclesiology before one decides to be a Christian. This is not to say that there is not a legitimate place for these inquiries and deliberations but that they are not the bases upon which the fundamental decision for or against faith is necessarily, or even most often, determined. For Holmer, as for Lewis, the "time-honored pattern that suggests that we must think and understand with a second-order scheme" is a false model when applied to Christianity.[33] Holmer sees the preponderance of such theoretical proposals as promulgating a situation where "we are invariably imprisoned in these large philosophical or quasi-theological views before we can speak about specific Christian issues," and from within this situation, it is "as if there is no primary language at all," and that "all apprehension and knowing of Christian things is via the theology or second-level discourse."[34]

Again, Holmer sees in Lewis a critical response to this issue in regard to the fundamentals of the Christian faith:

> The grand yet simple theological truths that Lewis has such strong concern for are actually the elementary and plain assertions that make up the gospel itself. These are the kerygma, the rudimentary components making up the evangel, summarized in the creed of the apostles. Lewis did not consider these to be theology in the modern sense, nor were these teachings to be thought of as second-order meditations upon the primary material. This group of elementary sayings were truly the "what," the elements; and they were for Lewis, not, in the ordinary senses, a point of view, an angle upon the facts, or an optional view.[35]

Whether or not Holmer agrees with the specifics of this view of the Apostles' Creed may be debated, but it is clear that he shares the basic sentiment

32. Ibid., 38.
33. Ibid., 102.
34. Ibid., 100.
35. Ibid., 98.

expressed here that distinguishes the kerygma from second-order discourse about it. His concern is to allow this basic "what" of Christianity to be what persons decide for or against rather than a particular systematic translation of it.

Beyond this, Holmer is suggesting that this misportrayal of the "what," the content of Christianity, results in an overemphasis on the teachings and a too narrowly defined sense of what constitutes the cognitive component of Christianity. As he writes:

> That shallow notion is that we first encounter some teachings, then ascertain whether they make sense—for example, whether they are true or false, meaningful, or relevant at all—then respond to them with our emotions, will, and behavior. This way of describing human living puts the theory first; the abstract definition of facts, rules, or duties is in the dominant position. Then the 'sense' is supposed to be chiefly in the teachings, while the rest—deeds, emotions, and willing—is part of the application or the practice. Then we get the familiar distinctions like theory and practice, teaching and use, abstract and concrete.[36]

The response to this fundamental critique, as Holmer notes was sometimes the case for Lewis, is that one is characterized as "naive" or "anachronistic," and the notion of what is seen to be a "theory-free" or "non-interpretive" core of the Christian faith is termed "literalistic" or even "anti-intellectual." But what Holmer is arguing in contrast to this theory-practice bifurcation is by now perhaps obvious, namely, "that people, not just words or teachings have to make sense" and "that lives can begin to make sense, via emotions, will virtues and thoughts, when all these things are under Christian nurture."[37] It is the view that there is a necessary correlation between the "how" of the faith and the "how" of the human self. And it is here that we come to the place of the description of another sort of "grammar," what Holmer sometimes calls the "grammar of life." It is this radically different perspective and pedagogy that he perceives in Lewis' work as a writer and Christian apologist, in Kierkegaard and even in Wittgenstein.

36. Holmer, *Making Christian Sense*, 75.
37. Ibid.

5. Nurturing Christian Character

We have earlier noted Holmer's view of the virtues as "habitual character traits" which function to help create and form a person's self-understanding and behavior. It is this interweaving of self-understanding and behavior that the term "character" is meant to suggest. In this sense, "character" denotes not simply the self as knower, but rather, the "whole person," as a "living synthesis of thought and pathos, of affection, will, and reflection, of purpose, hope, judgment and memory."[38] It is this whole person that Holmer seeks to address when he writes of making sense emotionally, morally, volitionally and intellectually. And it is the whole person that is addressed and taught, according to Holmer, by the Christian faith.

Part of this process of achieving an enduring sense of self-identity, of being formed as a person, of developing "character," as we have noted, consists for Holmer in understanding oneself as a moral agent. And it is through this discovery and the discipline provided by the virtues that one is further educated to what it means to be a self. In this context, we become different, according to Holmer, "by knowing more of who we are and what we want."[39] It is here that a kind of rationality, appropriate to the whole human person begins to take root and grow, enabling one to discover and connect with a larger rationality and the "objectivities" of life. As Holmer writes:

> By paying attention to the subject one discovers the object. Sown in subjectivity and reaped in objectivity. . . . All rational propensities are also a realized function of the human subject. . . . The point is one has to discover and learn to be rational. . . . After a while—if our lives are concentrated and serious—those sayings of a primary variety begin to be facts . . . When we have worked on our lives in a moral way, assessed and judged by the virtues and commands, we also erase those capacities which keep doubt alive.[40]

According to Holmer, there is a rationality and even objectivity accessed by what is often seen to be the realm of subjectivity, of emotion and interest. The language of these concerns—"of" ethics and "of" religion—is therefore, even as the language of feeling and conviction, also a language that addresses issues of fact and truth. But it is only this as it teaches and

---

38. Ibid., 101.
39. Holmer, *C. S. Lewis*, 105.
40. Ibid., 104–5.

forms one's perspective of oneself and the world. As Holmer writes concerning Christian teachings: "Rather, it supposes that getting those words on our lips will require that our whole consciousness and manner of looking at the world will also have to change. Thus, new emotions and feelings will be required, and a whole train of new passions and convictions will ensue. Then an appropriate way of thinking about what is the fact will also occur. By such means, we will also find the truth and know objective reality."[41]

What Holmer is suggesting here is that just as the virtues serve an educatory function in the life of one who follows them, so, too, Christian concepts and teachings work in the life of faith. In this sense, one is not merely educated to Christianity, but by it. Christianity, for Holmer, is not merely a set of teachings, but rather, like the virtues, a discipline that forms one's life and view of the world. It is the capacity of the Christian faith to help persons make sense of and with their lives that is Holmer's evangelical concern. In light of this concern his work—and the task of Christian theology—is to help elucidate "the conditions by which a person can forge his or her own life in a manner that is distinctively Christian."[42] In this sense, what Holmer says of Lewis applies to his own work, namely, that "he writes in such a way as to educate, literally to educe, in his reader most of the capacities and skills that he needs to become faithful, critical, understanding and, in brief, enabled and empowered."[43]

On the one hand, Holmer's analytic, descriptive task is undertaken as the "grammar of the language of faith." What the analysis of this grammar shows is that there is a necessary connection between the meaning of religious concepts and their appropriation, in the sense that to understand them is to be enabled and empowered by them. But in addition, Holmer also provides what amounts to a "grammar of the life of faith" or "morphology of the life of Christian belief" that demonstrates the use of religious concepts and teachings to create and nurture character. In reference to the latter, Holmer writes in *The Grammar of Faith*: "Just as religious concepts help one to see the world differently, as if it were God's and as if one were not alone, so they produce a new emotional tone appropriate to that appraisal of things. . . . Thus the teachings get bound up with attitudes, feelings, passions, and a host of behavior patterns, not indiscriminately but in patterned

41. Ibid., 106.

42. Holmer, *Grammar of Faith*, 153.

43. Holmer, *C. S. Lewis*, 110.

ways.[44]Although the evangelical task is a somewhat different one than that of a purely descriptive account of the grammar of faith, the latter serves to clarify the former. And one aspect that it clarifies is the relation between the "what" of the Christian faith and the "how" of both its appropriation and communication. As Holmer writes in regard to Kierkegaard's notion of two kinds of communication:

> In one and familiar instance, we communicate a bit of knowledge to someone else. That person understands, assents to what we have said, then that is the end of the matter. The other kind of communication Kierkegaard called "indirect," and he thought it peculiarly required in morals and religion. In the latter instances, we are also being taught to become something different. Here the requirements are new capabilities, new capacities altogether. In this case what one writer can do for another, his or her reader, is primarily to engender that kind of concern and self-regard in which the capability will grow up naturally and quickly.[45]

Holmer's presentation of the grammar of the language of faith describes a discourse that it used not merely to communicate information but to engender character. And when looking at Holmer's work as a whole it is clear that nurturing capacities and engendering character was also his goal. Indeed, those who knew Paul Holmer as a teacher experienced his pedagogy as a preeminent example of "indirect communication."

What we have tried to show, then, is that Holmer's work encompasses both a descriptive and evangelical intent.[46] The descriptive task of theology is not burdened by the weight of this larger purpose, but the evangelical task is informed by reflection on the language of faith. Where these two concerns meet is in the analysis of what Holmer terms the "morphology of the life of Christian belief." Here the perspectives of both Kierkegaard and Wittgenstein come into play. And yet, as we have seen, Holmer's concern is not to forward a particular school of thought, but rather to practice the way of thought exemplified in their writing. In keeping with the latter, Holmer undertakes his own process of reflection and, in so doing, makes a significant contribution to contemporary theology. By describing the grammar

---

44. Holmer, *Grammar of Faith*, 157–58.

45. Holmer, *C .S. Lewis*, 66.

46. Note our earlier discussion in the previous chapter of D. Z. Phillips' characterization of Holmer's "evangelical concern" as a "grammarian and guardian" of the faith.

of the language and life of faith, Holmer communicates something of the passion that is faith in God.

Conclusion: Making Sense with Language and Life

Early on in his *Making Christian Sense*, Holmer makes the simple statement that just as we need order and logic in our use of language to make sense, so, too, we need a similar rigor in order to make sense of our lives. In this simple way he suggests the analogy between the way grammar works in our use of language and what might be termed a "grammar of life." As he writes: "The person who helps you to make sense in talking does so by drawing on the many-sided and very informal grammar of our language and the equally complex and equally informal logic of our daily thought. These are embedded in human practices, in literature and ways of speaking; and they are not arbitrary."[47]

There are a number of significant points to note in this brief passage which may serve as summary of some of the fundamental themes of Holmer's thought. To begin with, Holmer suggests the way in which the grammar of our everyday language and thought is both complex and many-sided, and yet is, at the same time, "informal." The grammar of a language, while it may be explicitly delineated and analyzed, is ordinarily embodied in the ways that we learn to speak and do things in and with language. While learning grammar may be one part of our training in the language, such explicit learning normally occurs (at least in our native language) after one has already learned to do a variety of things in the language. In this sense, we already, by and large, have the grammar, although we may not be able to articulate the rules directly.

Secondly, despite the fact that the rules for using the language are embedded in the things we learn to do in our speaking and the like, this does not mean that the rules are mysterious and hidden, or that they are arbitrary. In particular, the fact that the rules of the language predate one's use of it means that one is part of a larger community engaged in making sense, or, at the least, in trying to make sense. And the way that one makes sense in the language, although some looseness of application may be allowed, is to follow the rules and conventions that comprise the grammar.

Both of these seemingly minor points, suggested in simply drawing the analogy between language use and life, are implied in Holmer's use of

---

47. Holmer, *Making Christian Sense*, 8.

the term "grammar." In addition, although the analogy is drawn between language and life, to speak of the language and "making sense" is already to suggest the connection between language and life, the connection between what we say and what we do in and with language. For it is to recognize that what we ordinarily mean when we speak of "making sense" is that people use language to make sense (or fail to), rather than the language itself. It is, I suggest, something akin to this fairly straightforward description that characterizes Holmer's work both as philosopher and theologian. For he seeks both to help us "make sense" in our language—with its words and concepts, names and all the rest—*and* to help us "make sense" in regard to the non-linguistic uses and practices that comprise the larger context of language and our lives.

More specifically, in appropriating Wittgenstein's remark about "theology as grammar," Holmer also directs our attention away from an exclusive focus on how our words (in this case, our concepts and beliefs) correspond to the world of facts, and by invoking the term "grammar" helps us ask how the facts of our lives might more fully correspond to our beliefs. Another way of putting it is to say that Holmer redirects the philosophical issue of "reference." Instead of the primary issue being "to what do our religious beliefs refer?" Holmer directs our attention to "how" they refer, that is, to how they refer believers. For in the case of religious faith, the grammatical—the theological—issue concerning "reference" is less about proving that our beliefs refer to God than learning how to refer our lives to God.

If our language use is to make sense, then, it is not merely a matter of using words correctly, but, on the one hand, having something to say, and on the other, seeing the connection between language and life, indeed, seeing that there is a connection between our words and actions. If our lives are to make sense, we need to be formed by the language and practices of ethical and religious concern. Indeed, Holmer believes that a recovery of moral sensitivity is essential to a "recovery of the capacity to believe in God."[48]

Lastly, Holmer's work calls us to attend once more—both in philosophical analysis and in theological reflection—to "ordinary" language. It is this focus on language in the vernacular and the first-order language of faith that is the hallmark of Holmer's way of doing philosophy and theology. In regard to theology in particular, he calls for a focus on the language that Christian people naturally speak and "the ordinary discourse in which

48. Holmer, *C. S. Lewis*, 114.

moral, passional and momentous concerns are initially couched."[49] It is this same concern with the adequacy and importance of the vernacular that energizes his critique of the tendencies in both theology and philosophy to generate theories, assume generalities and impose a univocal view of rationality.

In these ways, and others, Holmer returns philosophy and theology to the complex, informal and yet ruled character of human language and life. While the proclivity of contemporary theologians to seek metaphysical and ontological foundations for their work and to propose elaborate self-referential theological conceptualities and systems of meaning seems in no way abated, the lasting contribution of Paul L. Holmer's thought is perhaps yet to come to fruition. One of his students, Richard H. Bell, has understood Holmer's work under the rubric of the "grammar of the heart."[50] As he writes:

> When a person speaks of God or of matters of moral worth, that person is not preoccupied with the nature of propositional claims, rather he or she speaks as an ordinary person trying to find words to witness to what may be understood of a human self. This is no easy task when the very idea of a self is isolated from mutual concern, shared practices and a common life. Finding 'heart enough to be confident' in our time is often a lonely task.[51]

Paul Holmer carried out what was, no doubt, a sometimes lonely task. Yet, in describing the "grammar of the heart" and seeking to communicate it, he touched the minds and the hearts of discerning readers. As a writer and theologian, and perhaps even more importantly as a churchman and teacher, the range of issues that he engaged and the intellectual rigor—what I think is rightly characterized as the wisdom—that he brought to these issues, continues to influence a whole generation of his students. It is the legacy of a "certain shape of thought, a 'way' and a 'how' of thinking."[52]

49. Ibid., 96.
50. Bell, *Grammar of the Heart*.
51. Ibid., xxiv.
52. Holmer, *C.S. Lewis*, 9.

Bibliography

Books by Paul L. Holmer

Holmer, Paul L. *C. S. Lewis: The Shape of His Thought and Faith*. New York: Harper & Row, 1976.

———. *Communicating the Faith Indirectly: Selected Sermons, Addresses, and Prayers*. Edited by David J. Gouwens and Lee C. Barrett III. The Paul L. Holmer Papers 3. Eugene, OR: Cascade, 2012.

———. *The Grammar of Faith*. San Francisco: Harper & Row, 1976.

———. *Making Christian Sense*. Philadelphia: Westminster, 1984.

———. *On Kierkegaard and the Truth*. Edited by David J. Gouwens and Lee C. Barrett III. The Paul L. Holmer Papers 1. Eugene, OR: Cascade, 2012.

———. *Philosophy and the Common Life*. College of the Pacific Philosophy Institute 10. Stockton, CA: Fitzgerald, 1960.

———. *Theology and the Scientific Study of Religion*. Minneapolis: T. S. Denison, 1961.

———. *Thinking the Faith with Passion: Selected Essays*. Edited by David J. Gouwens and Lee C. Barrett III. The Paul L. Holmer Papers 2. Eugene, OR: Cascade, 2012.

———. *Youth Considers Doubt and Frustration*. Camden, NJ: J. T. Nelson, 1967.

Articles and Sound Recordings by Paul L. Holmer

———. "About Being a Person: Kierkegaard's *Fear and Trembling*." In *Kierkegaard's Fear and Trembling: Critical Appraisals*, edited by Robert L. Perkins, 81–99. Tuscaloosa: University of Alabama Press, 1981.

———. "About Black Theology." *Lutheran Quarterly* 28/3 (1976) 231–39.

———. "About Liturgy and Its Logic." *Worship* 50/1 (1976) 18–28.

———. "About Our Capacity to Talk." *The Philosophy Forum* 7/4 (1969) 29–42.

———. "About Religious Consciousness." *Lutheran Quarterly* 23/2 (1971) 138–49.

———. "About Understanding." Unpublished manuscript. Yale University Divinity School (1977?). Reprinted in Paul L. Holmer, *Thinking the Faith with Passion: Selected Essays*, edited by David J. Gouwens and Lee C. Barrett III, 163–88. The Paul L. Holmer Papers 2. Eugene, OR: Cascade, 2012.

———. "Atheism and Theism: A Comment on Academic Prejudice." *Lutheran World* 13/1 (1966) 14–25.

Bibliography

———. "Buber and Christianity." Sound recording. Undated forum/panel with Leslie Higgins and George Lindbeck. Yale University Divinity School Library, Record Group No. 53, Box 87.

———. "Christianity and the Truth." *Lutheran Quarterly* 9/1 (1957) 33–41.

———. "Contra the New Theologies." *Christian Century* 82/11 (March 17, 1965) 329–32.

———. "Crisis in Rhetoric." *Theological Education* 7/3 (1971) 208–15.

———. "Ecumenics and Theology." *Lutheran Quarterly* 21/2 (1969) 154–64.

———. "Evolution and Being Faithful." *Christian Century* 84/47 (1967) 1491–94.

———. "Faith and Community: A Christian Existential Approach." *Lutheran Quarterly* 12/2 (1960) 179–80.

———. "Four Existentialist Theologians: A Reader from the Works of Jacques Maritain, Nicolas Berdyaev, Martin Buber, and Paul Tillich." *Lutheran Quarterly* 12/1(1960) 69–70.

———. "A Fragment of Thought about Feminism, Language and Church." *Reflection* 82/2 (1985) 14–16.

———. "Historical Research and Christianity." *Encounter* 20/3 (1959) 367–72.

———. "Indirect Communication: Something About the Sermon (with References to Kierkegaard and Wittgenstein)." *Perkins School of Theology Journal* 24/2 (1971) 14–24.

———. "Karl Heim and the Sacrifice of Intellect." *Lutheran Quarterly* 6/3 (1954) 207–19.

———. "Kierkegaard and Ethical Theory." *Ethics* 63 (1953) 155–70.

———. "Kierkegaard and Logic." *Kierkegaardiana* 2 (1957) 25–42.

———. "Kierkegaard and Philosophy." In *New Themes in Christian Philosophy*, edited by Ralph M. McInery, 13–33. Notre Dame: University of Notre Dame Press, 1968.

———. "Kierkegaard and Radical Discipleship: A New Perspective." *Journal for the Scientific Study of Religion* 9/1 (1970) 67–70.

———. "Kierkegaard and Religious Propositions." *Journal of Religion* 35 (1955) 135–45.

———. "Kierkegaard and the Nature of Philosophy." Sound recording. University of California, 1960.

———. "Kierkegaard and the Sermon." *Journal of Religion* 37 (1957) 1–9.

———. "Kierkegaard and the Truth." PhD diss., Yale University, 1945.

———. "Kierkegaard and Theology." *Union Seminary Quarterly Review* 12/3 (1957) 23–31.

———. "Kierkegaard as Critic." *Religion on Campus* 1 (1965) 4–7, 10.

———. "Language and Theology." *Harvard Theological Review* 58/3 (1965) 241–61.

———. "Law and Gospel Re-Examined." *Theology Today* 10/4 (1954) 471–81.

———. "The Logic of Preaching." *Dial* 4 (1965) 205–13.

———. "The Meaning of Religious Language." Sound recording. San Francisco Theological Seminary, 1960.

———. "Metaphysics and Theology: The Foundations of Theology." *Lutheran Quarterly* 17/4 (1965) 291–315.

———. "The Minister, a Reconsideration: Meditatio, Oratio, Tentatio." *Reflections* 72/3 (1975) 3–9.

———. "The Nature of Religious Propositions." In *Religious Language and the Problem of Religious Knowledge*, edited by R. E. Santoni, 233–47. Bloomington: Indiana University Press, 1968.

———. "The Nature of Theology." *Journal of Religious Thought* 9/2 (1952) 37–145.

———. "On Being Steadfast: Jesus Christ, the Same . . ." *Reflections* 71/1 (1973) 8–11.

———. "On Criticizing the Church." *Theology Today* 26/3 (1969) 326–34.

———. "On Understanding Kierkegaard." In *A Kierkegaard Critique*, edited by Howard A. Johnson and Niels Thulstrup, 43–54. New York: Harper, 1962.

———. "Paul Tillich and the Language about God." *Journal of Religious Thought* 22/1 (1965–66) 35–50.

———. "Paul Tillich: Language and Meaning." *Journal of Religious Thought* 22/2 (1965–1966) 85–106.

———. "Philosophical Criticism and Christology." *Journal of Religion* 34 (1954) 88–100.

———. "Polanyi and Being Reasonable: Some Comments in Review of *Intellect and Hope*." *Soundings* 53/1 (1970) 95–109.

———. "Post-Kierkegaardian Remarks about Being a Person." In *Kierkegaard's Truth*, edited by Joseph Smith et al., 3–22. New Haven: Yale University Press, 1981.

———. "Religious Experience and Truth: A Symposium." *Theology Today* 20/4 (1964) 583–85.

———. "Restless Spirit." *Religious Education* 71/6 (1976) 664–65.

———. Review of *The Dilemma of Contemporary Theology: Prefigured in Luther, Pascal, Kierkegaard, Nietzsche*, by Per Lonning. *Journal of Religion* 45 (1965) 167–69.

———. Review of *Faith and Community: A Christian Existential Approach*, by Clyde Holbrook. *Lutheran Quarterly* 12/2 (1960) 179–80.

———. Review of *In Search of the Self: The Individual in the Thought of Kierkegaard*, by Lukas Miller. *Dialog* 1 (1962) 80.

———. Review of *Kierkegaard and Radical Discipleship*, by Vernard Eller. *Journal for the Scientific Study of Religion* 9/1 (1970) 67–70.

———. Review of *Meditations from Kierkegaard*, edited and translated by T. H. Croxall. *Journal of Religion* 36 (1956) 285.

———. Review of *Theological Foundation of Law*, by Jacques Ellul. *Lutheran Quarterly* 13/3 (1961) 274–75.

———. "Scientific Language and the Language of Religion." *Journal for the Scientific Study of Religion* 1/1 (1961) 42–55.

———. "Some Reflections About Law and Gospel." *Lutheran Quarterly* 11/2 (1959) 124–34.

———. "Something About What Makes It Funny." *Soundings* 57/2 (1974) 157–74.

———. "Søren Kierkegaard." In *Christian Ethics: Sources of the Living Tradiation*, edited by Waldo Beach and H. Richard Niebuhr. New York: Ronald, 1955.

———. "Spirit in the Thought of Nicholas Berdyaev." *Lutheran Quarterly* 3 (1951) 3–22.

———. "Stewards of Mysteries." *Cross Currents* 5/1 (1955) 32–38.

———. "Theological Foundation of Law." *Lutheran Quarterly* 13/3 (1961) 274–75.

———. "Theology and Belief." *Theology Today* 22/3 (1965) 358–71.

———. "Theology and Education." *Religious Education* 60 (1965) 28–31.

———. "Theology and Happiness." *Reflections* 67/3 (1970) 3–7.

———. "Twentieth Century Religious Thought: The Frontiers of Philosophy and Theology, 1900–1960." *Union Seminary Quarterly Review* 19/1 (1963) 69–73.

———. "Use of Devotional Literature." *Journal of Biblical Religion* 22 (1954) 99–103.

———. "Wittgenstein and the Self." In *Essays on Kierkegaard and Wittgenstein*, edited by Richard H. Bell and Ronald E. Hustwit, 10–31. Wooster, OH: College of Wooster, 1978.

———. "Wittgenstein and Theology." *Reflection* 65/4 (1968) 2–4.

Bibliography

―――. "Wittgenstein and Theology." In *New Essays in Religious Language*, edited by Dallas High, 25–35. New York: Oxford University Press, 1969.
―――. "Wittgenstein: 'Saying' and 'Showing.'" *Neuen Zeitschrisft fur Systematisch Theologie* 22/3 (1980) 222–35.

Other Works

Allen, Diogenes. Review of *C. S. Lewis: The Shape of His Faith and Thought*, by Paul L. Holmer. *Princeton Seminary Bulletin* 1/4 (1978) 285–86.
Austin, J. L. *How to Do Things with Words*. Edited by J. O. Urmson and Maria Shia. Cambridge, MA: Harvard University Press, 1975.
Ayer, Alfred Jules. *Language, Truth and Logic*. 2nd ed. New York: Dover, 1946.
Bell, Richard H., ed. *The Grammar of the Heart: New Essays in Moral Philosophy and Theology*. San Francisco: Harper & Row, 1988.
―――. "Wittgenstein and Descriptive Theology." *Religious Studies* 5 (1969) 1–18.
Bell, Richard H., and Ronald L. Hustwit, eds. *Essays on Kierkegaard and Wittgenstein: On Understanding the Self*. Wooster, OH: College of Wooster, 1978.
Burgess, Andrew, J. *Passion, "Knowing How," and Understanding: An Essay on the Concept of Faith*. Missoula, MT: Scholars, 1975.
―――. Review of *C. S. Lewis: The Shape of His Faith and Thought*, by Paul L. Holmer. *Dialog* 18 (1979) 237.
Burrell, David B. Review of *The Grammar of Faith*, by Paul L. Holmer. *Journal of Religion* 61 (1981) 211–12.
―――. Review of *The Nature of Doctrine*, by George Lindbeck (1984b). *Union Seminary Quarterly Review* 39 (1984) 322–24.
Cathey, Robert Andrew. *God in Postliberal Perspective: Between Realism and Non-Realism*. Burlington, VT: Ashgate, 2009.
Cavell, Stanley. *Must We Mean What We Say? A Book of Essays*. Cambridge: Cambridge University Press, 1976.
Currie, Thomas. Review of *The Grammar of Faith*, by Paul L. Holmer. *Interpretation* 33 (1979) 308–11.
Diem, Hermann. *Kierkegaard's Dialectic of Existence*. Translated by Harold Kight. Edinburgh: Oliver and Boyd, 1959.
Downey, John K. *Beginning at the Beginning: Wittgenstein and Theological Conversation*. Landham, MD: University Press of America, 1986.
Evans, Donald. *The Logic of Self-Involvement*. London: SCM, 1963.
Flew, Anthony. *God and Philosophy*. New York: Harcourt, Brace and World, 1966.
―――, ed. *Logic and Language (First and Second Series)*. Garden City, NY: Doubleday, 1968, 1973.
Flew, Anthony, and Alasdair McIntyre, eds. *New Essays in Philosophical Theology*. London: SCM, 1955.
Frei, Hans. *The Eclipse of Biblical Narrative: A Study in Eighteenth and Nineteenth Century Hermeneutics*. New Haven: Yale University Press, 1974
―――. *The Identity of Jesus Christ: The Hermeneutical Basis of Dogmatic Theology*. Philadelphia: Fortress, 1975.
Frye, Roland M. Review of *C. S. Lewis: The Shape of His Faith and Thought*, by Paul L. Holmer. *Theology Today* 34 (1977) 231–32.

Hazelton, Roger. Review of *C. S. Lewis: The Shape of His Faith and Thought*, by Paul L. Holmer. *Andover Newton Quarterly* 18/3 (1978) 254–55.

High, Dallas M. *Language, Persons, and Belief: Studies in Witggenstein's Philosophical Investigations and Religious Uses of Language*. New York: Oxford University Press, 1967.

Hunsinger, George. "Postliberal Theology." In *The Cambridge Companion to Postmodern Theology*, edited by Kevin J. Vanhoozer, 42–57. Cambridge: Cambridge University Press, 2003.

Kerr, Fergus. *Theology after Wittgenstein*. Oxford: Blackwell, 1986.

Kierkegaard, Søren. *The Concept of Dread*. Translated with an introduction and notes by Walter Lowrie. Princeton: Princeton University Press, 1957.

———. *Concluding Unscientific Postscript*. Translated by David F. Swenson. Princeton: Princeton University Press, 1941.

———. *Edifying Discourses: A Selection*. Edited with introduction by Paul L. Holmer. Translated by David F. Swenson and Lillian M. Swenson. New York: Harper, 1958.

———. *Fear and Trembling and The Sickness Unto Death*. Translated with introduction and notes by Walter Lowrie. Princeton: Princeton University Press, 1954.

———. *The Diary of Søren Kierkegaard*. Edited by Peter Rhode. New York: Citadel, 1987.

———. *The Journals of Kierkegaard*. Translated, selected, with an introduction by Alexander Dru. New York: Harper and Row, 1959.

———. *Philosophical Fragments*. Translated by David Swenson; translation revised by Howard H. Hong. Princeton: Princeton University Press, 1962.

———. *The Point of View for My Work as an Author: A Report to History and Related Writings*. Edited by Benjamin Nelson. New York: Harper & Row, 1962.

———. *Stages of Life's Way*. Translated by Walter Lowrie. New York: Schocken, 1967.

———. *Training in Christianity*. Translated with an introduction and notes by Walter Lowrie. Princeton: Princeton University Press, 1944.

———. *Works of Love: Some Christian Reflections in the Form of Discourses*. Translated by Howard Hong and Edna Hong. New York: Harper & Row, 1962.

Lewis, C. S. *The Abolition of Man*. New York: Macmillan, 1947.

———. *Christian Reflections*. Edited by Walter Hooper. Grand Rapids: Eerdmans, 1967.

———. *The Four Loves*. New York: Harcourt Brace Jovanovich, 1960.

———. *God in the Dock*. Edited by Walter Hooper. Grand Rapids: Eerdmans, 1970.

———. *Mere Christianity*. New York: Macmillan, 1952.

———. *Studies in Words*. Cambridge: Cambridge University Press, 1960.

Lindbeck, George. *The Nature of Doctrine: Religion and Theology in a Postliberal Age*. 25th anniv. ed. Lousville: Westminster John Knox, 2009.

MacDonald, Dursten. Review of *The Grammar of Faith*, by Paul L. Holmer. *Anglican Theological Review* 62 (1980) 182–84.

Madren, E. Dale. Review of *C. S. Lewis: The Shape of His Faith and Thought*, by Paul L. Holmer. *Duke Divinity School Review* 42/3 (1977) 205–6.

Nielsen, Kai. "Wittgensteinian Fideism." *Philosophy* 42 (1967) 191–209.

———. "Wittgensteinian Fideism Again: A Reply to Hudson." *Philosophy* 44 (1969) 63–65.

Phillips, Dewi Z. *Faith After Foundationalism*. New York: Routledge, 1988.

———. *Faith and Philosophical Enquiry*. London: Routledge, 1970.

———. "Grammarians and Guardians." In *The Grammar of the Heart: New Essays in Moral Philosophy and Theology*, edited by Richard H. Bell, 21–35. San Francisco: Harper & Row, 1988.

Bibliography

————. *Religion Without Explanation*. Oxford: Blackwell, 1976.

Placher, William. "Revisionist and Postliberal Theologies and the Public Character of Theology." *The Thomist* 49 (1985) 392–416.

Purtill, Richard L. Review of *The Grammar of Faith*, by Paul L. Holmer. *Christian Scholar's Review* 8/3 (1978) 272–73.

Robbins, Jerry. Review of *The Grammar of Faith*, by Paul L. Holmer. *The Christian Century* 96/7 (1979) 225.

Roberts, Robert C. "The Independence of Theology." Review of *The Grammar of Faith*, by Paul L. Holmer. *Reformed Journal* 30/2 (1980) 29–32.

Ryle, Gilbert. *The Concept of Mind*. New York: Barnes and Noble, 1949.

————. *Philosophical Arguments*. Oxford: Clarendon, 1945.

Sherry, Patrick. "Learning How to Be Religious: The Work of Paul Holmer." *Theology* 77 (1974) 81–90.

————. *Religion, Truth and Language Games*. New York: Barnes and Noble, 1977.

Shideler, Mary M. Review of *C. S. Lewis: The Shape of His Faith and Thought*, by Paul L. Holmer. *New Review of Books and Religion* 1/7 (1976) 7.

Stiefel, R. E. Review of *C. S. Lewis: The Shape of His Faith and Thought*, by Paul L. Holmer. *Anglican Theological Review* 60/2 (1978) 254–55.

Strawson, P. F. "On Referring." *Mind* (1950) 320–44; reprinted in *Logico-Linguistic Papers*. New York: Barnes and Noble, 1971.

Thiselton, Anthony C. *The Two Horizons: New Testament Hermeneutics and Philosophical Description with Special Reference to Heidegger, Bultmann, Gadamer and Wittgenstein*. Grand Rapids: Eerdmans, 1980.

Tilley, Terrence. Review of *The Grammar of Faith*, by Paul L. Holmer. *Theological Studies* 40 (1979) 541–43.

Toulmin, Stephen. *Human Understanding*. Princeton: Princeton University Press, 1972.

Vanhoozer, Kevin J., ed. *The Cambridge Companion to Postmodern Theology*. Cambridge: Cambridge University Press, 2003.

Waissmann, Frederick. "Language Strata." In *Logic and Language (First and Second Series)*, edited by Anthony Flew, 226–47. Garden City, NY: Doubleday, 1965.

Wells, David. Review of *The Grammar of Faith*, by Paul L. Holmer. *Christian Scholar's Review* 10/1 (1980) 84–85.

West, Cornell. Review of *The Grammar of Faith*, by Paul L. Holmer. *Union Seminary Quarterly Review* 35/3–4 (1980) 279–85.

Whittaker, John H. *The Logic of Religious Persuasion*. New York: Lang, 1990.

Wittgenstein, Ludwig. *Culture and Value*. Edited by G. H. von Wright. Translated by Peter Winch. Chicago: University of Chicago Press, 1980.

————. *Last Writings on the Philosophy of Psychology*. Edited by G. H. von Wright and Hiekki Nyman. Translated by C. G. Luckhardt and Maximillian A. E. Aue. Chicago: University of Chicago Press, 1982.

————. *Lectures and Conversations on Aesthetics, Psychology and Religious Belief*. Compiled from notes taken by Yorick Smythies, Rush Rhees, and James Taylor. Edited by Cyril Barrett. Berkeley: University of California Press, 1966.

————. *On Certainty*. Edited by G. E. M. Anscombe and G. H. von Wright. Translated by Denis Paul and G. E. M. Anscombe. New York: Harper & Row, 1969.

————. *Philosophical Grammar*. Edited by Rush Rhees. Translated by Anthony Kenny. Berkeley: University of California Press, 1974.

———. *Philosophical Investigations.* Translated by G. E. M. Anscombe. New York: Macmillan, 1958.

———. *Philosophical Remarks.* Edited by Rush Rhees. Translated by R. Hargreaves and R. White. Oxford: Blackwell, 1964.

———. *Tractatus Logico-Philosophicus.* Translated by D. F. Pears and B. F. McGuinness. New York: Humanities, 1961.

———. *Zettel.* Edited by G. E. M. Anscombe and G. H. von Wright. Translated by G. E. M. Anscombe. Berkeley: University of California Press, 1970.

Wood, Charles M. Review of *The Grammar of Faith*, by Paul L. Holmer. *Perkins Journal* 32/4 (1979) 52–53.

———. *Vision and Discernment: An Orientation in Theological Study.* Atlanta: Scholars, 1985.

www.ingramcontent.com/pod-product-compliance
Lightning Source LLC
Chambersburg PA
CBHW060343100426
42812CB00003B/1100